AMBROSE BIERCE

THE LITERARY WEST SERIES

SAN FRANCISCO

AMBROSE BIERCE

The Making of a Misanthrope

BY RICHARD SAUNDERS

CHRONICLE BOOKS

FOR TODDIE WITH LOVE

Printed in the United States of America.

LIBRARY OF CONGRESS CATALOGING IN PUBLICATION DATA

Saunders, Richard, 1947–
Ambrose Bierce: the making of a misanthrope.
(The Literary West series)
Bibliography: p. 104
INCLUDES INDEX.
1. Bierce, Ambrose, 1842–1914?
2. Authors, American – 20th century – Biography. 3. Authors, American – California – Biography. 4. California – Intellectual life.
I. Title. II. Series
PS1097.Z5S28 1984 813'.4 [B] 84-17606
ISBN 0-87701-297-0 (pbk.)

PHOTO AND ILLUSTRATION CREDITS

Courtesy, The Bancroft Library: pages 13, 90

The Ambrose Bierce Collection, Department of Special Collections, Stanford Univeristy Libraries: pages 74, 75, 77, 79, 84, 88, 98, 100

Courtesy, Mrs. Grace Bussing: page 18

Courtesy, The California State Library: page 58

Courtesy, Harrison Memorial Library: page 87

Courtesy, The Henry E. Huntington Library: page 49

Stanford University Archives: pages 28, 72

Gary Waters: page 43

EDITING
Carey Charlesworth

COMPOSITION
Type by Design

CHRONICLE BOOKS
870 Market Street
San Francisco, California 94102

CONTENTS

ACKNOWLEDGMENTS

My sincere thanks go out to the staffs
of the Henry E. Huntington Library in
San Marino; the Stanford University
Library; the California Historical
Society in San Francisco; the Bancroft
Library at the University of Cali-
fornia, Berkeley; the Napa County
Historical Society; the California State
Library in Sacramento; the Silverado
Museum in Saint Helena; the Marin
County Historical Society in San
Rafael and the Harrison Memorial
Library in Carmel.

PREFACE

WHEN AMBROSE BIERCE
wandered off at the age of seventy-one into the chaos of revolutionary Mexico he created one of the most profound literary mysteries of
this century. The last letter anyone received from him (postmarked
Chihuahua City and dated December 26, 1913) revealed his intentions of traveling to Ojinaga by rail to join the forces of Pancho Villa.
After that, silence . . . . and following the silence there has been
endless speculation as to his fate. The mystery was born and has
refused to die. In a life filled with a special brand of irony it's not too
surprising that "Bitter Bierce" is almost as well known today for his
enigmatic exit from this life as he is for his writings.

Oddly enough, my interest in Ambrose Bierce began, in my
sophomore year of college, when I saw an Academy Award–win-
ning short-subject film based on his story "An Occurrence at Owl
Creek Bridge." Looking back, I can now appreciate that this unlikely
cinematic introduction to a man who made his reputation by the
printed word was absurdly apropos. It seems a twist the old master
himself would have reveled in, since the majority of his fiction is shot
through with highly ironic (and often existential) situations.
Regardless, my curiosity had been sparked, and I soon found myself
on a seemingly uncontrollable Bierce binge—devouring his short
stories on war, horror, ghosts and madness; breezing through his
newspaper columns and epigrams of sardonic wit; and lingering,
sometimes cringing, over his acid-tongued "definitions" from The
Devil's Dictionary.

Several years later I became intrigued with the life of Ambrose Bierce. I soon found that his ill-fated journey across the Mexican border, which launched him into literary mythology, has been sensationalized in magazine articles about him and often overemphasized in full-length biographies. If the earlier writers of these works were anxious to solve a mystery they might better have turned their attention to the dark, unexplained sources of the author's cynical misanthropy. They might also have looked to a rapidly changing California, and how it shaped and ultimately embittered this true product of the Golden State. This, then, is what I have set out to accomplish—for Bierce's California years not only span the great majority of his productive career but also hold the key to his exceedingly complex character.

In traveling around the state to visit the spots where Bierce and his family lived I've found his ghost to be a restless and elusive one. From his lofty mountain retreats above Santa Cruz, the Napa Valley and Los Gatos to his homes in San Rafael and Saint Helena only the house in Saint Helena (where he was at best a part-time resident from 1886–89) is formally recognized as the author's former residence. In January of 1984 The Ambrose Bierce House opened its doors as a bed-and-breakfast inn after six months of meticulous restoration. Other than this recent addition to Bierceiana there are no plaques, no monuments, no streets named after the writer to pin down his memory. And yet he would have probably wanted it that way, for Bierce took a certain perverse pleasure in creating something of a riddle of himself.

One of the most eccentric men of letters ever produced by this country, Ambrose Bierce was a California original. A flawed genius with little faith in mankind, he combined his satiric wit with an almost demonic vengeance to deflate individual egos, institutions and accepted customs more powerfully than any other writer had done before his day or has since. He is chiefly remembered for his stories of the Civil War (by far the best ever written by a veteran of that conflict), his eerie tales of horror and his excursions into the world of black humor; but Bierce's accomplishments as a serious journalist with a finely tuned social conscience are grossly underrated. He never stopped fighting hypocrisy, racial prejudice and political corruption wherever he found it.

And yet the mystery surrounding his disappearance will

probably forever overshadow the tumultuously productive life of Ambrose Bierce. Following his name, any encyclopedia or biographical dictionary you pick up queries the date his life ended: 1842–1914? My hope is to move up the question mark to before these relatively meaningless dates, and to answer it . . . Ambrose Bierce? Who was Ambrose Bierce?

I
SAN FRANCISCO:
A NEW
BEGINNING

LATE IN 1866, WITH THE
bloody horrors of the Civil War one year over, twenty-four-year-old
Ambrose Bierce traveled by Sacramento River boat into the San
Francisco Bay, both figuratively and literally on the verge of a new
and quite unexpected phase of his life. Although the colorful and
exotic city by the Bay held a certain fascination for him, the young
brevet major's visit there was official military business. He intended,
upon proceeding to the Presidio, to receive written confirmation of
his promotion to a captaincy in the peacetime army.

At the age of nineteen, a mere four days after Lincoln issued
his call for volunteers, Ambrose Bierce had been the second man in
Meigs County, Ohio, to enlist in the Union Army. As a private in
Company C, Ninth Indiana Infantry, he saw action at Shiloh, Mur-
freesboro, Nashville, Franklin and Chickamauga and was cited
several times for bravery. Wounded in the head at Kenesaw Mountain, he seemingly returned from the dead, and served as Gen. W. B.
Hazen's trusted topographical engineer until the close of the war. In
1866 he accompanied General Hazen on a mapping and inspecting
expedition through the Far West with the understanding that an
officer's commission would await him in San Francisco. However,
the abundance of officers left over from the war was so great that
almost all of those who were to stay in the regular army had to take

reduction in rank. Bierce soon confronted the shocking news that all he could expect was a commission as a second lieutenant in the Fifth Infantry.

A young man possessing a tremendous sense of pride as well as a vulnerable ego, Bierce had been caught in the sticky web of military red tape. Realizing that a second lieutenancy was all he could expect from what he perceived to be an ungrateful government, the gravely insulted soldier chose to totally ignore the commission, neither accepting nor declining it formally. With little experience other than as a soldier, plus a two-year stint as a printer's devil in Indiana while still a teenager, he nevertheless sensed that journalistic opportunity in the young and vibrant metropolis was wide open, and this gave him the confidence to consider a newspaper career. It is said that his ultimate decision whether to accept the military position or to pursue the vague pipedream of a journalistic career rode on the simple toss of a coin. The coin came up heads, and to the good fortune of many besides Bierce journalism won the toss.

While a lesser man might have felt stranded and apprehensive in a city like San Francisco, Bierce met the challenge head on. For more than a year he supported himself by working as a night watchman at the Sub-treasury Building while by day studying the classics and developing his writing skills. Through an extensive and methodically planned course of academic study that emphasized classical literature and history, the youthful exsoldier embarked on an ambitious regimen of self-education. All of his energies were directed toward this one goal. There was no turning back.

AMBROSE GWINETT BIERCE

was born June 24, 1842, in Meigs County, Ohio. The tenth child of Marcus and Laura Bierce, Ambrose was four years old when the family moved near Warsaw, Indiana. He was brought up with the hell fire of Calvinism licking at his heels, and he had no real affection for any members of his family except Albert, his next older brother, who also served in the Civil War and later settled in California. Ambrose's father, being dominated equally by his religion and his wife, cared to claim only two things as his own—the whimsical idea of naming each of his thirteen offspring beginning with the letter A, and the largest private library in the town. Although Ambrose took refuge in the library during those early years he was nevertheless deeply scarred by the ignorance and extreme insularity of the community surrounding him. A loner with a vivid imagination, he was not popular at school and was only an average student. Early on he felt out of step with his contemporaries. In truth, the vast majority of people rubbed him the wrong way, from his "predictably idiotic" fellow students to his own family members, whom he would later coldly describe as "unwashed savages."

During these formative years Ambrose Bierce's character was greatly determined by his stern parents, who never thought of sparing the rod and showed precious little affection for their children. Quite naturally the severe upbringing affected each child differently, and Ambrose, the most sensitive of the lot, reacted by becoming a rebel. It was his feeling that there were simply too many children in the Bierce home, and he would later write (in "The Love of Country," *The Collected Works*) that "the human heart has a defi-nite quantity of affection. The more objects it is bestowed upon, the less each object will get." The emotional distance he felt from his family soon gave way to the alienation he felt from the townspeople of Warsaw, then a mere village of some three hundred people. Although it was the county seat Warsaw was nevertheless a primi-tive and uninspiring town, and young Ambrose felt antagonistic toward its citizens, whom he considered ignorant farmers hiding behind their repressive religion. He found his only refuge in the serenity of nature. Northern Indiana was then covered with forests, lakes and rivers; Ambrose found canoeing on nearby Goose Lake and hiking along the banks of the Tippecanoe River some three miles from town preferable to plowing in the fields and attending prayer meetings. This emotionally rejuvenating link with nature would play an important role throughout his life, and Bierce himself made his stance clear when he wrote "I pity the dunces who don't under-stand the speech of earth, heaven and ocean."

By 1867 Bierce was living at the Russ House, a four-story hotel that spanned Montgomery between Pine and Bush streets, and was becoming as well known for his literary aspirations as for his striking physical appearance. At six feet tall he carried himself with a rigid military erectness and took great pride in his clothing as well as keeping his thick reddish-blonde hair neatly trimmed. Despite these striking features, the first thing usually noticed about him was his icy blue eyes, half-hidden under thick, frosty brows. Bierce's dashing good looks were the perfect embodiment of the newly emerging image of a cosmopolitan San Francisco. The ragtag characters of the

AMBROSE BIERCE AS A YOUNG COLUMNIST SHORTLY
AFTER HE EARNED THE TITLE OF "THE WICKEDEST MAN IN
SAN FRANCISCO."

gold rush were quickly being replaced by sophisticated businessmen, and it was clear that the end of the so-called Western frontier was at hand. Along with this change came a rapidly growing demand on the part of the public for social and political satire in their daily newspapers and, in general, a more worldly outlook. The need was met with the highly personalized style of rough-and-ready journalism that flowed from the pens of such then-novice writers as Mark Twain, Bret Harte, Joaquin Miller, Ina Coolbrith, Prentice Mulford and Charles Warren Stoddard. The name of Ambrose Bierce soon would be added to this select list; he began placing verse, short articles and essays in highly regarded newspapers and literary journals such as the *Golden Era,* the *Californian* and the *Alta California,* as early as 1868.

That Bierce was in the right place at the right time is certain, but much of his luck he made for himself. The greenest four-leaf clover he plucked was San Francisco's *News Letter*, a modest eight-page financial weekly aimed at businessmen. Founded in 1856 by an Englishman, Frederick Marriott, the *News Letter* reported the news, commented on local affairs and set aside one page for a satirical column called the "Town Crier." Bierce had greatly enjoyed the column under the editorship of an Englishman named James W. Watkins, with particular fondness for the uncivil and totally blasphemous attacks it leveled on other newspapers, journalists, poets, politicians and local ministers; and in the summer of 1868 Bierce had had a number of his own witty contributions to the column published. When Watkins determined to leave San Francisco to further his journalistic career in New York, he and Marriott searched for someone versed in the "art of abuse" to take over the page, and Watkins, contacting the newcomer, discovered that Bierce's cynicism rivaled his own. He took Bierce under his wing and introduced his protégé to the satire of Swift, Thackeray and Voltaire in hopes that the newly published writer could learn to effectively control his savagery and polish his style. Watkins quickly realized that the column was tailor made for the young cynic's biting social commentary, and in December of 1868, at the age of twenty-six, Ambrose Bierce became editor of the "Town Crier" and never looked back.

Although it is safe to assume that at this stage in his career Bierce was concerned with maintaining the "Town Crier" tradition of attacking hypocrisy and sham where he found it, some historians have missed the mark in theorizing that his acidity and sarcastic brand of humor were dictated by the established format of the column. Of course, he must have been eager to please his new employer as well as his readers; but even so Bierce's devilishly flippant tone and mastery of the satirical art simply cannot be written off as clever marketing technique. Anyone who reads even these early offerings can't help but notice that the improvements in the column under Bierce's editorship were beyond technique—there was an unmistakable streak of genuine hostility running through every line. The misanthropy, more evident than ever, immediately brings Dean Swift to mind. Bierce was a born satirist with a monumental chip on his shoulder, and San Franciscans quickly learned to love the abuse he so eloquently heaped on the deserving.

Soon the fireworks from Bierce's particularly sardonic column lit up the San Francisco scene. The highly subjective style and fearless attacts on hypocrisy won the new "Town Crier" a huge audience. Not only were his targets so varied the public seldom knew where the young cynic might next strike, but there was a feeling that his complete lack of inhibition was forever on the edge of being out of control. The electricity in these early efforts simply forced people to stand up and take notice. Public figures, unworthy authors and corrupt institutions felt the sting of his satire, and everyone (from the mayor to the members of the Olympic Athletic Club, from the chief of police to the smug membership of the Pioneer Society) was subject to the prick of his often sharp pen. Many thought him a man gone wild. Although he first leaned heavily on the tall-tale brand of humor born on the Western frontier, Bierce's quips and uncensored observations soon transcended the established journalistic rules of the day. People felt, with good reason, that he was capable of turning on anyone, and within a year he was dubbed "the wickedest man in San Francisco." Bierce's reaction to all this attention was typically blasé. He advised people to continue selling shoes, selling pancakes or selling themselves; "as for me, I sell abuse."

The abuse dished out by Bierce, mostly deserved and always entertaining, frequently targeted organized religion. Although ribbing churches and preachers was a long-time *News Letter* practice, Bierce, especially, seemed to delight in these assaults. Ever since he had revolted against the Calvinist camp meetings of his childhood Bierce's violent condemnation of evangelical religion and the unChristian behavior of self-avowed Christians was a favorite theme. In flaunting his belligerent irreverence for the church he often pointed out the hypocritical actions of its members, as in the following item, which concerned the persecution of the "heathen" Chinese living in San Francisco and the questionable behavior of "civilized" Christians:

On last Sunday afternoon a Chinaman passing guilelessly along Dupont Street was assailed with a tempest of bricks and stones from the steps of the First Congregational Church. At the completion of this devotional exercise the Sunday-scholars retired within the hallowed portals of the sanctuary, to hear about Christ Jesus, and Him crucified.

While God-fearing men were horrified at such blasphemy and preachers publicly called him a "laughing devil," Bierce reacted by claiming he had suddenly seen the light, and even offered a prayer of repentance:

O, Lord, who for the purposes of this supplication we will assume to have created the heavens and the earth before man created Thee; and who, let us say, art from everlasting to everlasting; we beseech Thee to turn Thy attention this way and behold a set of the most abandoned scalawags Thou has ever had the pleasure of setting eyes on. . . . But in consideration of the fact that Thou sentest Thy only-begotten Son among us, and afforded us the felicity of murdering him, we would respectfully suggest the propriety of taking into heaven such of us as pay our church dues, and giving us an eternity of exalted laziness and absolutely inconceivable fun. We ask this in the name of Thy Son whom we strung up as above stated. Amen.

From his blasting of religion to the overtly sexist attitude he maintained to his hatred of politicians, Bierce was unpredictable in his wrath. In a column written in the late 1860s he put forward a now-famous tongue-in-cheek defense for a candidate for the Board of Education accused of consorting with an Oriental prostitute by arguing that the candidate would certainly reform if elected because "no respectable harlot who cares for her reputation would continue her acquaintance with a man who had been elected to the Board of Education." He also routinely commented on freak accidents, suicides and homicides, often startling an aghast readership by adding macabre asides. "The Italians continue their cheerful national recreation of stabbing one another," he reported glibly, "On Monday evening one was found badly gashed in the stomach, going about his business with his entrails thrown over his arm." Bierce was at least impartial in ladling out his castigations. He spared no one and let it be known that he was not concerned with what others called fair play; if he used stereotypes, he also attacked them.

The outright bluntness of Western journalism allowed Bierce to develop as a satirist, and by 1870 his reputation as a vicious yet uniquely talented cynic had spread across the country. Indeed, his near-sadistic personal attacks and brutal handling of many sensitive topics made him a great many enemies, and in a town barely emerging from the Wild West era he was constantly being threatened. It was even rumored that bets had been taken on his longevity. With his reputation as a superb marksman during the war, his imposing military posture and a fearless icy stare for any foe, he was never challenged to a duel. But when you consider that two far less caustic newspapermen, named Edward Gilbert and James King of William, were both shot dead in San Francisco, it isn't hard to understand Bierce's insistence on carrying a revolver at all times.

BIERCE BECAME THE BAD

boy of San Francisco—the man everyone loved to hate. His public behavior during this period seems to have rivaled his journalistic reputation, and it's quite conceivable that he was the archetypical "media man," known equally well for his craft and his personal exploits. He was cautiously admired as a celebrity in both literary Russian Hill and in the social circles of Nob Hill. With his strikingly handsome features and thick moustache he quickly gained a reputation as a lady killer, possessing a decidedly macho type of animal magnetism. More than one admiring female claimed she could "feel" his presence from ten feet away, and Bierce took full advantage of this fact. Always meticulously dressed, he was one of the most dashing men in the city, and his unsavory, slightly evil reputation made him all the more attractive to the majority of women.

Although the young Bierce was one of the most eligible bachelors in San Francisco, he was also extremely evasive. Once he mastered the social graces necessary to infiltrate respectable society when it suited his needs, he could be at his best behavior in order to meet a particularly beautiful woman of "good breeding," while the following day he might very well be enjoying the warm hospitality of one of the city's finest bordellos and the day after that he could be found at the bar of the Russ House playfully joking with some hard-drinking fellow writers. Known as an "eminent tankard-man" even at this early date, Bierce was known to go on wild alcoholic binges that, coupled with his deep love of pranks, often resulted in hilarious escapades. One of these booze-inspired incidents, involving Bierce, poet Charles Warren Stoddard and writer Jimmy Bowman, founder of the famed Bohemian Club, actually led to wide newspaper coverage on its own merit. After drinking the night away one New Year's Eve the three men decided that they would strike Christianity a fatal blow by pulling down the huge wooden cross that was erected by the pious on a hill near Golden Gate Park during the Christmas season. Equipped with ropes and several additional flasks of whiskey the trio managed to lasso the cross but tugged in vain to tear the symbol of blind devotion to the ground. In their drunken state they decided that if they tied the ropes around their shoulders and waists and then pulled together like a mule team their joint effort would surely topple the cross. However, either the whiskey or the cross was too strong, for their clumsy efforts accomplished nothing more than to hopelessly tangle together the three crusading atheists and bound to the cross they all passed out in a state of exhaustion. When they were discovered the following morning the faithful rescuers wasted no time in drawing the obvious and highly ironic moral.

At the same time

that Bierce periodically scorched the pages of the *News Letter* with antifeminists quips he fell hopelessly in love with the lovely Mary Ellen "Mollie" Day. The young and attractive only daughter of a prosperous Forty-Niner, Mollie met Ambrose during one of his

MOLLIE BIERCE SHORTLY AFTER HER MARRIAGE TO AMBROSE IN 1871.

sporadic, chameleon like forays into polite society in San Rafael, across the Bay in Marin County, and he was immediately mesmerized by her youthful charm, vivaciousness and unexpected wit. He soon found himself seriously courting her, much to the horror of her domineering mother, who, obsessed with her position in San Francisco society, cringed at the thought of a lowly-journalist son-in-law with a wicked reputation and a penchant for attacking the Best People in print. Although Mrs. Day loudly voiced her objections to the love match, both Mollie and her father, Holland Day, spoke up in favor of the union. For once Mrs. Day's self-centered social aspiration lost out to her highly romantic daughter and the unpretentious nature of her rich husband. Mollie and Ambrose were married on Christmas Day of 1871, and Captain Day, as he was then known, came down from his mining enterprise in Utah to give his daughter away with wholehearted blessings. From that point on Bierce would value his father-in-law above most men. The wealthy yet down-to-earth Captain Day surprised everyone with his generous wedding gift to the newlyweds — an all-expenses-paid trip to England for an extended honeymoon.

After a brief respite in San Rafael Bierce bid a hasty farewell to the faithful readers of his "Town Crier" column, and, in April of 1872, set out for England with his bride. Ambrose Bierce knew that this was his chance to make a name for himself beyond the confining limits of San Francisco.

2
BITTER BIERCE
AND THE
"ARGONAUT"
YEARS

BIERCE'S HEAD WAS

filled with visions of worldwide recognition and lasting fame when he and Mollie arrived in England in the summer of 1872, and within a few months his name was added to those of a small colony of California-based writers working in London. All of these writers from the romantic Far West, including Mark Twain, Joaquin Miller and Prentice Mulford, caused a great stir abroad, and it wasn't long before Bierce came to the realization that the "American rage" among the literati in that city was at its peak. But whereas the reputation of Mark Twain had already been established with the publication of "The Celebrated Jumping Frog of Calaveras County," *The Innocents Abroad* and *Roughing It,* and Joaquin Miller was already considered the premier poet of California, Ambrose Bierce walked into London as an unknown freelance journalist who decided to make a name for himself on foreign soil. He was one of the few Americans in history to actually accomplish this remarkable literary feat and would later consider his three-year stay in England the happiest and most prosperous period of his life.

The newlyweds found London both intellectually stimulating and "the cleanest of cities." While the handsome young couple

turned heads wherever they went, it was Ambrose's odd combination of a lucid mind and dark cynicism that ultimately attracted
the London literary crowd. A letter of introduction from *News
Letter* publisher Marriot was all he needed to infiltrate the Bohemian
ranks of Fleet Street, and he and Mollie sampled the local restaurants and concert halls for a time, although Bierce gradually began
spending most of his time pubcrawling with writers and editors. He
did make valuable business contacts through what he called "the
gang" at various journalistic hangouts, and the smart set in London
was also enchanted by the charismatic young Westerner and his
social graces.

Using the unlikely pen name of Dod Grile, Bierce began
writing humorous sketches for Tom Hood's weekly newspaper *Fun*
and for James Mortimer's *Figaro*. Both papers were well suited to
Bierce's mordant outlook, and soon the likes of William E. Glad-
stone, the intermittent prime minister, began praising his dry sense
of humor and proclaimed him a genius. His fame and popularity grew
swiftly, and in 1872 his first book appeared, a collection of his newspaper writings entitled *The Fiend's Delight*. From that time on things
moved at a dizzying pace. In December the Bierces had their first
child, a son named Day. Much to Ambrose's regret, the summer of
1873 brought Mollie's mother to Hampstead (where the family
moved to lessen the effects of the harsh London fog on Ambrose's
battle with asthma, which would be lifelong); it was a ten-month
stay, and he was soon braving even the damp fogs to escape his
mother-in-law's critical eye. In the same year a second book, *Nuggets
and Dust*, was published, and 1874 brought a second son, named
Leigh, and yet another collection of newspaper sketches in book
form entitled *Cobwebs from an Empty Skull*.

The years abroad were busy and somewhat hectic for Bierce,
who pushed himself unrelentingly to produce copy for as many as
five publications at the same time. His reward came, however, with
the wide recognition he had strived for but could not obtain in
California. He must have felt he had indeed arrived when he was the
guest of honor at a lavish banquet given by the famous White Friars'
Club of Fleet Street. That the young satirist was held in such high
esteem is evident by his seating at the head of a table where two
other American writers strongly linked with California also were
honored—Mark Twain and Joaquin Miller. Bierce, hailed as "one of
the most originial and daring humorists this age has produced," felt ill

at ease the entire evening due to his relationship with the other two writers. Having met Twain only once in San Francisco in 1868, as the Town Crier Bierce had taken him to task when he married the daughter of a wealthy man in 1870, by writing:

Mark Twain, who, whenever he has been long enough sober to permit an estimate, has been uniformly found to bear a spotless character, has got married. It was not the act of a desperate man—it was not committed while laboring under temporary insanity . . . it was the cool, methodical, culmination of human nature working in the heart of an orphan hankering for some one with a bank account to caress . . . Well, that genial spirit has passed away; that long, bright smile will no more greet the early bar-keeper, nor the old familiar "chalk it down" delight his ear. Poor Mark! he was a good scheme, but he couldn't be made to work.

Evidently Twain took the piece in the spirit of good fun in which it was intended, or, if not, perhaps he had the pleasure of the last laugh when Bierce himself married a rich man's daughter less than two years after he wrote the tongue-in-cheek condemnation. Regardless, both men were amiable during the dinner and actually found solace in their mutual embarrassment concerning the antics of "the poet of the Sierras," Joaquin Miller. To their horror Miller looked and dressed exactly how the English imagined a typical Californian should appear—full beard, shoulder-length hair, a buckskin jacket, red sash, boots and spurs. Even his eccentric garb took second place to his behavior that night, for toward the end of the dinner he took to galloping around the table on all fours, smoking two cigars at once, and he ended the evening's entertainment by picking up a fish by the tail and swallowing it whole. Both Bierce and Twain tried to ignore these antics, but the English were thrilled to have finally met "a real Californian." In later years Bierce would sum up Miller's literary output by quipping "he rewrites his life from reading dime novels."

As an American journalist Bierce performed an unprecedented feat in London in supporting himself and his family for more than three years on money earned solely by freelance writing. His literary criticism, satirical newspaper pieces and books so wittily and courageously dissected man's universal folly that he came to be called "Bitter Bierce"—a nickname that stuck with him for the rest of his life. But by 1875 Bitter Bierce was spending so much time wining and dining with the Fleet Street Bohemia that Mollie, bored with the lonesome Warwickshire countryside to which they had recently moved, tending two infant sons as well as playing nurse to her husband's frequent hangovers finally had enough. She was terribly homesick and wanted to return to America with her children to visit her mother for a few months. It was not a serious estrangement between the couple by any means, but shortly after Mollie's departure in the spring Ambrose let it be known that he missed his wife and sons desperately. Aside from loneliness he was also suddenly plagued with an undiagnosed illness, which was probably the combined result of too much hard work, overdrinking and a lack of sleep as well as his ever-present asthma. Regardless of the source of his brief illness, Bierce received a major shock that summer when he received a letter from Mollie explaining that she could not return as planned because she was pregnant again and wanted to have their third child on American soil. It has never been determined whether Mollie knew of her condition before leaving England or if she realized that she was going to have another child and thought that if she could get back to America, even on the pretense of a visit, the impending birth would impel her husband to return to California. The end result of the letter, however, is well known. In September of 1875 Ambrose Bierce hastily left his beloved England and a month later arrived in San Francisco.

It was less than a

month after Bierce reached San Francisco that Mollie gave birth to a daughter, named Helen. Now unemployed and the father of three, he came back to a city in the midst of a crushing financial depression that had it roots in the 1873 panic of the New York Stock Exchange. While hard times were hitting the little man, however, nothing could faze the money kings of the Southern Pacific Railroad. The Big Four—Leland Stanford, Collins P. Huntington, Charles Crocker and Mark Hopkins—had finally succeeded in clenching an iron fist around the entire state. Their railroad monopoly, real estate investments and mining and shipping interests gave them the power to manipulate corrupt politicians and to multiply their fortunes as well as those of the men who cooperated with their master plan. California was being split apart by the economic fault line of haves and have nots. Luxurious mansions dripping with architectural gingerbread sprouted on Nob Hill while thousands of men lost their jobs and the lucky ones took wage cuts of 50 to 60 percent. The impression of impending doom was heightened dramatically when William

Ralston's rock-solid Bank of California was forced to close down and, days later, its founder committed suicide.

The returning Bierce was thrown into the eye of this economic hurricane. Although he had a verbal agreement with Marriott before leaving for England that if he should return to San Francisco he could have his "Town Crier" job back, neither of them could have anticipated the current depression. Funds were simply not available to rehire Bierce. However, Marriott was sympathetic to the plight of his former columnist and agreed to buy some free-lance articles as well as a unique satiric feature called "The Demon's Dictionary." The "dictionary" was actually a list of forty-eight words with accompanying definitions in a highly caustic vein. Some thirty years later one entire volume of Bierce's twelve-volume *Collected Works* would be built on this premise and indeed become one of his most popular works, now known as *The Devil's Dictionary*. As for this early, ground-breaking effort, Bitter Bierce more than lived up to his famous nickname:

Piety, n. Reverence for the Supreme Being, based upon His supposed resemblance to man.

Pocket, n. The cradle of motive and the grave of conscience.

Prejudice, n. A vagrant opinion without visible means of support.

Present, n. That part of eternity dividing the domain of disappointment from the realm of hope.

Queen, n. A woman by whom the realm is ruled when there is a king, and through whom it is ruled when there is not.

Quill, n. An implement of torture yielded by a goose and commonly wielded by an ass.

Rational, adj. Devoid of all delusions save those of observation, experience and reflection.

Respectability, n. The offspring of a liaison between a bald head and a bank account.

Road, n. A strip of land along which one may pass from where it is too tiresome to be to where it is futile to go.

Rum, n. Generically fiery liquors that produce madness in total abstainers.

Saint, n. A dead sinner revised and edited.

Senate, n. A body of elderly gentlemen charged with high duties and misdemeanors.

Vote, n. The instrument and symbol of a freeman's power to make a fool of himself and a wreck of his country.

Unfortunately, making a living in San Francisco by freelancing was next to impossible and Bierce was forced to humble himself by getting on the government payroll again, this time landing a job at the Assay Office of the Mint. The times were so hard that he knew he was lucky to be employed anywhere. And he was only able to land the job because of his prior experience with the government and the pull of his brother, Albert, who left Indiana after the war and had been working at the Mint for several years while living in Oakland. For over a year Bierce sulked and dutifully went to work at the Assay Office, feeling his three years in England spent building a reputation had suddenly gone down the drain. Worse yet, they were living on Harrison Street and were constantly visited by Mollie's mother, who lived just a few blocks away on Market Street. Often his only relief from the irritating Mrs. Day, who greatly contributed to the Bierce's growing domestic tensions, was to visit the Bohemian Club and spend the night soaking up the literary atmosphere and trading witticisms with his fellow writers.

WHILE BIERCE WORKED

at the Mint and contributed a scant amount of material to various local journals, the city of San Francisco was straining under the weight of radical reform and the rise of trade unionism. Almost all of those fortunate enough to hold jobs were unionized, while the jobless in their growing discontent took vent in hatred of the Chinese, channeled by the rabble-rousing efforts of Denis Kearney and his Workingmen's Party. As in most economic depressions there was a psychological need on the part of the unemployed masses to find a suitable scapegoat, and the immigrant Chinese workmen fit the bill perfectly. After laboring on the most dangerous section of the Central Pacific Railroad and in 1869 seeing the country finally linked by rail, many of the hard-working Chinese came to San Francisco to compete for jobs. Ironically, it was another immigrant, Irish drayman Denis Kearney, who formed the Workingmen's Party in order to put a stop to the relative success of the Chinese workers, who had already proved from their railroad days that they would work harder than Caucasians for less money. Kearney's solution was to run the 116,000 Chinese out of America, and he took to making radical soapbox speeches on an open sandlot next to City Hall, shouting the soon-familiar slogan "the Chinese must go!"

Kearney's fiery demagoguery overstepped its bounds when he began making antiwealth and anticapitalism speeches aimed at the millionaires on Nob Hill and promised to wrest government from the hands of the wealthy. As Kearney's speeches became more violent his devoted followers, the great majority of them being burly long-shoremen and assorted unemployed laborers, armed themselves to the teeth, predicting that the city would be leveled to ashes. Kearn-eyism, as it came to be called, began to frighten most people. Slogans such as "bread or blood" were chanted during the sandlot gather-ings, and the legislature was threatened with "hemp"–hanging. Before long an equally violent solution to Kearneyism began to take shape with the formation of a vigilance committee known as the "Pickhandle Brigade." Ready to stand up to the radicals of the Work-ingmen's Party at a moment's notice, they were well armed with pick handles as well as rifles. It made no great impression on these self-appointed overseers that Kearney's racist thugs were busily storing bundles of dynamite, which they planned to drop on the residents of Chinatown from manned balloons, but when they threatened that white politicians and millionaires would soon be strung up from lamp posts, the pickhandles were brought out in a strong show of united opposition.

Into this dangerous match up of paramilitary forces came a new weekly newspaper, *The Argonaut*, which was well financed by railroad and real estate interests and dedicated to the downfall of Kearneyism. The founder of the paper was Frank Pixley, a wealthy Republican who was a strong supporter of Leland Stanford and was a former U.S. district attorney. With future political aspirations of his own, Pixley was a shrewd opportunist who had his sights set on nothing less than the governor's mansion in Sacramento. To achieve this end he hired an able journalist named Fred Somers as coeditor and relied heavily on his knowledge of publishing as well as his talents as a writer. Both men agreed that the paper would need a circulation-boosting columnist and knew there was only one man for the job – Ambrose Bierce. With a sizeable and extremely loyal fol-lowing from his days on the *News Letter* in San Francisco and his prestigious journalistic triumphs in London, Bierce was just the type of writer a new paper needed, and he jumped at the opportunity to leave the Mint and return to weekly journalism. The first issue of *The Argonaut* appeared in March of 1877, and Bierce soon found himself taking on all editorial responsibilities, training a staff of writers and contributing a weekly column called "Prattle." The content of the new column was similar to his earlier "Town Crier" page, taking deadly aim at politics, clergymen, actors, suffragettes and misguided writers with satirical arrows dipped in poison. No friend of Kearney, he tore into the political agitator with unbridled venom and delighted his readers as well as the paper's conservative owner. However, Pixley's frequent request to attack the Irish Catholic population fell on deaf ears, and Bierce was soon at odds with the man's racist policies. The Prattler was actually a liberal when it came to the subject of race and nationality, and he often lashed out at the injustices suffered by the Chinese, blacks and Jews of San Francisco. In his view all of mankind was a hopelessly botched experiment devised in hell, and the stupidity of every soul on earth had nothing whatsoever to do with ancestry.

Bierce's considerable reputation and his high regard for the art of satire were the two factors that led to the immediate acceptance of The Argonaut. Although San Francisco had more than its share of newspapers and weekly literary journals, with Bierce assuming editorial control the new paper became an overnight success. Unfortunately, trouble was on the horizon. Pixley's continued insistence on frequent anti-Irish attacks in print and Bierce's intention of gradually turning the paper into a literary journal of lasting importance that would include insightful criticism were in constant conflict, and the two men locked horns over editorial policy for years. Had Bierce's name not carried such tremendous weight with readers he would have been fired early on, but his increasing popularity with the public both forced Pixley to keep him on and gave the Prattler the freedom to speak his mind on all matters without regard to official policy. Over the years the two men were often at each other's throat, Bierce publicly attacking some of the owner's influential personal friends in print and Pixley routinely being absent on payday.

Apart from the bothersome infighting at the offices of The Argonaut, San Francisco was still plagued with the violence of the frontier, and many journalists and editors felt the need to be armed at all times. Bierce continued his practice of packing an Army Colt on the streets and was soon keeping it within reach on his desk as well. He was actually forced to pull it in self-defense during one altercation, when the irate husband of actress Katie Mayhew stormed Bierce's office and threw him against a glass-fronted bookcase after Bierce called her "a charming blackguard" in his column.

A PANORAMA OF THE PRATTLER'S SAN FRANCISCO
TAKEN FROM THE CALIFORNIA STREET HILL BY
EADWEARD MUYBRIDGE IN 1878.

Such tense and highly volatile confrontations, which were common, were taken much more seriously when one of the major newspaper publishers on the West Coast, Charles de Young of the *Chronicle*, was shot dead by the son of San Francisco's mayor for printing a derogatory article about the attacker's father. In any case, Bierce went about business as usual and lampooned anyone he pleased without regard to his own personal safety, as evidenced by the following comment on the death of one of Oakland's most powerful citizens: "The personal property of the late Anthony Chabot, of Oakland, has been ordered sold. This is a noble opportunity to obtain Senator Vrooman."

JUST WHEN BIERCE'S CAREER

in journalism was again on the upswing his marriage showed serious signs of deterioration. After moving to San Rafael in hopes that the milder climate might lessen the severity of Ambrose's asthma attacks, the Bierce household was again invaded by Mollie's troublesome mother. Mrs. Day's visits increased in length until she simply moved in permanently, claiming that she couldn't bear to be across the Bay from her darling daughter. In truth the Harpy like Mrs. Day caused a good deal of trouble by constantly reminding Mollie that her husband was too argumentative, overbearing and moody and spent too much of his time away from home. Soon Bierce was spending so much time in San Francisco that he seemed like a visitor at his own home in San Rafael. He finally realized why his father-in-law, rich as he was, lived the life of a recluse in remote mining camps. But even without the bothersome complications caused by Mrs. Day, Bierce's freewheeling life-style had been decidely nondomestic from the start. For a father of three infants he was distant; he found the job of parenting a relentless nuisance. While his artistic, self-centered temperament would allow for an occasional moment of fun by bouncing baby Helen on his knee or playing with his sons, on the whole Bierce found children irksome and a distraction from his work. Even with the birth of his first son in England he had been curiously devoid of the normal chest-beating pride often evident in a new father. As for babies in general, he wrote in *Nuggets and Dust* that they are "excellent to soothe one's ruffled temper, for you may readily relieve your feelings by pinching them, and they can't tell."

To ease the pressure brought about by his unhappy domestic life and his continuing war against Kearneyism, Bierce took the time to pull off a successful literary hoax. In the summer of 1877 he and co-conspirators T. A. Harcourt and William Rulofson published a thin volume entitled *The Dance of Death* under the joint pseudonym William Herman. The book itself was a brilliant tongue-in-cheek condemnation of the waltz. The inspired hoaxers denounced the waltz as "an open and shameless gratification of sexual desire and a cooler of burning lust." However, in their carefully calculated over-zealousness the trio went into great detail and not only branded the waltz as "lascivious" but attacked the lewd nature of the dance in such suggestive and titillating terms that the book promptly sold eighteen thousand copies on the West Coast alone. Amazed at the effectiveness of their little deception, the authors gleefully sat back and watched the ensuing fireworks. While much of the general public was properly shocked at the inherently sexual imagery, clergymen were divided and argued bitterly among themselves over whether the book was a deeply moral tract or a shameless open invitation to the world to join in the sinful dance. Regardless of one's point of view everyone seemed to be talking about it, and Bierce himself helped sales along by attacking it in his column as

a high-handed outrage, a criminal assault upon public modesty, an indecent exposure of the author's mind. . . . the poisoned chalice critics are gravely commending to the lips of good women and pure girls. Their asinine praises may perhaps have this good effect: William Herman may be tempted forth to disclose his identity. Then he can be shot.

The end result was that *The Dance of Death* was a surprising commercial success and an unexpected source of joy to the hoaxers. After the book was strongly endorsed by a Methodist Church conference the men celebrated for twenty-four hours straight, and toasted time and again its financial rewards as well as the hypocritical, unquestioning stupidity of what Bierce liked to call "that immortal ass, the average man."

BIERCE WAS SOON BACK

to fighting Kearney, and with more ferocity than ever after the demagogue led a two-day seige of Chinatown, cracking heads, looting homes and burning Chinese-owned businesses. Kearney was thrown in jail for a mere two weeks and then released. From that point forward Bierce devoted himself to destroying the Workingmen's Party and its radical leader in the pages of *The Argonaut*. While the strength of the party was underestimated by most people (they eventually won state assembly seats and elected the bizarre Reverend Isaac Kalloch mayor of San Francisco), Bierce continually apprised his readers that the injustice and violence associated with Kearneyism could very well swing their way in the future. Within a year the nonviolent public withdrew its support of the Workingmen and created a tremendous backlash that shook the party to its foundations. A rise in employment and serious splits and power struggles within the party further undermined its credibility. Even the *Call* and the *Chronicle*, two leading newspapers that had sympathized with Kearney, withdrew their support. When Kearney himself was accused by his colleagues of selling out to the capitalists and misusing party funds, Bierce swooped down on him like a hawk with a bead on a wounded mouse. Keaney's descent from political power was astonishingly rapid. After being ousted from the presidency of the party he attempted to join several other political parties, without success, and within a few years he retired from politics entirely. In the meantime the Workingmen's Party lost the San Francisco election of 1880, hit bottom and shortly thereafter fell apart. Although Bierce could finally claim victory in his personal war against Kearney, the dangerous demagogue had won many a battle, most of them at the cost of the Chinese, who were merely pawns in a game called politics (and whose immigration was soon to be halted under the Chinese Exclusion Act).

Oddly enough, Denis Kearney's sudden fall from power aggravated problems at *The Argonaut*. Pixley and Bierce had had absolutely nothing in common other than their mutual hatred for Kearney, and when he ceased to be a threat the two men grew to despise each other personally as well as politically. Bierce's fierce code of ethics and rigid sense of honor would never let him sell out to anyone on any issue, whereas Pixley could be bought at a moment's notice when it was to his ultimate advantage. Of course, from Pixley's point of view Bierce fueled the discord. On occasion Bierce would embarrass him by lampooning one of the editor's influential friends in the column, although for the Prattler Pixley's ranting over it amounted to little more than a source of amusement.

Still overburdened with editorial duties, Bierce managed occasionally to try his hand at a poem or short story for the paper, but he always felt these early literary efforts were neither appreciated nor understood by Pixley. He was probably right. When a grateful poet came into *The Argonaut* offices to personally thank Pixley for publishing a sonnet the poet had contributed, the editor looked up from his desk in bewilderment and asked "What's a sonnet?"

Bierce finally tired of Pixley's ignorance in literary matters, his political corruptness and his tardy paychecks. By the middle of 1879 Bierce had relieved himself from his full-time "Prattle" duties and became an only-occasional contributor to *The Argonaut* while exploring the money-making possibilities in the newly opened mining territory in the Black Hills of the Dakota Territory. In no time at all he had caught the gold fever and announced that he would quit the ulcer-riddled newspaper business for good, in order to strike it rich in the badlands of Dakota.

3
THE DEVIL'S
ADVOCATE

AMBROSE BIERCE HAD BEEN
aflame with gold fever ever since the government announced that
the Dakota Territory was being reopened to settlers and miners. By
the spring of 1880 his knowledge of assaying (acquired at the Mint)
and his expertise as a topographical engineer (drawing on his war
experience, he had made a map of the Black Hills country that was
published by the San Francisco firm of A. L. Bancroft and Company
in 1877) had landed him a top position with the Black Hills Placer
Mining Company. By July he found himself in Rockerville, a violent
and untamed town situated in the western part of today's South
Dakota. A mere four years earlier the Black Hills had played host to
the annihilation of George Armstrong Custer and 264 soldiers of the
Seventh Cavalry at the battle of the Little Big Horn, and also the
senseless murder of Wild Bill Hickok, the legendary scout and
lawman who was shot in the back of the head while playing poker in
a bar in Deadwood. It was not what you would call a civilized region
even by Bierce's standards. He soon found himself hiring Wells Fargo
sharpshooters to accompany the twice-weekly stage carrying
money out of nearby Deadwood because it was robbed so often by
desperate outlaws.

Surrounded by miners, gamblers, prostitutes, murderers and
shady businessmen, Bierce must have known early on that this
frontier boomtown was far from a safe bet. For a few months he was
kept busy supervising the construction of a seventeen-mile box

---

flume, which tapped the Spring Creek reservoir and led to the dry diggings. Everything seemed to be on schedule, and miners and stockholders alike were confident that the bonanza would be uncovered any day. The big day never came. Instead the poorly organized company ran out of capital, and by early fall construction operations were at a standstill. Bierce's urgent letters to the New York office demanding additional funds to meet the payroll of the mine were shrugged off while lawyers fought in a last ditch effort to save the company. Finally Bierce took it upon himself to travel to New York to secure the cash, but by the time he arrived he learned that the company was insolvent. His dream of a great bonanza was a bust. In December he left New York for San Francisco, his spirit and hopes of easy riches shattered and his distrust of mankind strengthened.

The humiliation of returning to San Francisco as a failure with a flat pocketbook was nothing compared to the glaring "I told you so" greeting Bierce was subjected to by his mother-in-law. The mining venture might have been a fiasco, but he determined to rid himself and his family of the overbearing Mrs. Day once and for all. He immediately moved his wife and three children into a modest house in the sparsely populated Fort Mason district, on a hillside over-looking the Bay.

Convinced that he had solved his domestic quandary, Bierce confidently assumed that he would be rehired and welcomed with open arms at *The Argonaut*. Not so. Both Pixley and Somers agreed that Bierce, in essence, caused more trouble than he was worth. While his popular "Prattle" column drew some readers it had re-pelled many others, and the owners and editors alike agreed that if they could get along without him during his six-month sojourn in the mining fields they could get along without him forever. For several months Bierce was forced to make ends meet by freelancing for various newspapers; then in January of 1881, his hard luck finally changed, and he was hired by the *Wasp* (a satirical weekly "born to sting") to take over editorial duties and continue his "Prattle" column. An established humorous and political magazine, the *Wasp* was a hotbed of social commentary that was decidedly antirailroad. Owner Charles Webb Howard and managing editor Edward C. Macfarlane both agreed that Bierce's unbridled journalistic expres-sion would bring thousands of new readers to the *Wasp*.

Disillusioned by his failure in the Black Hills and genuinely surprised by the cold ingratitude demonstrated by Frank Pixley at *The Argonaut*, Bierce's cynicism reached new heights. His column wasted no time in attacking "Mr. Pigsley of the Hogonaut," Bierce assuring his readers that he had made *The Argonaut* and now he would destroy it. Ambrose Bierce was not a forgiving soul. He held life-long grudges, and even Pixley's death some years later inspired nothing more than irreverent bluntness. Read Bierce's epitaph:

HERE LIES FRANK PIXLEY — AS USUAL

At the *Wasp* the Prattler was again in his element, publically executing everyone who displeased him with sadistic slashes of the pen. When he criticized a book or a poem that didn't measure up to his own literary standards, one *Wasp* edition alone could witness the destruction of a literary career. He also meted out ruthless attacks on politicians; snide, backhanded swipes at big business; and brutal assaults on rival San Francisco newspapers. Again, he declared open season on organized religion, and he satirized clergymen by writing about the double standards and self-righteousness of his favorite preacher — "Brother Mortificationoftheflesh J. Mucker."

The satirical feature that had first appeared in the pages of *The Argonaut* entitled "The Demon's Dictionary" was renamed "The Devil's Dictionary" in the *Wasp*, and these cynical mock definitions entertained readers over the entire course of Bierce's five-year editorship. Now beginning with the letter *A* and working his way forward to *P*, the point where he had mysteriously begun his dictionary years earlier, Bierce took such obvious pleasure and applied such fine wit to redefining words that he often induced the readers to reexamine the validity of their own thinking.

Accordion, n. An instrument in harmony with the sentiments of an assassin.

Air, n. A nutritious substance supplied by a bountiful Providence for the fattening of the poor.

Alone, adj. In bad company.

Archbishop, n. An ecclesiastical dignitary one point holier than a bishop.

Clairvoyant, n. A person, commonly a woman, who has the power of seeing that which is invisible to her patron — namely, that he is a blockhead.

Cynic, n. A blackguard whose faulty vision sees things as they are, not as they ought to be. Hence the custom among the Scythians of plucking out a cynic's eyes to improve his vision.

Dentist, n. A prestidigitator who, putting metal into your mouth, pulls coins out of your pocket.

Duty, n. That which sternly impels us in the direction of profit, along the line of desire.

Evangelist, n. A bearer of good tidings, particularly (in a religious sense) such as assure us of our own salvation and the damnation of our neighbors.

Faith, n. Belief without evidence in what is told by one who speaks without knowledge, of things without parallel.

Famous, adj. Conspicuously miserable.

History, n. An account mostly false, of events mostly unimportant, which are brought about by rulers mostly knaves, and soldiers mostly fools.

Immigrant, n. An unenlightened person who thinks one country better than another.

Joss-Sticks, n. Small sticks burned by the Chinese in their pagan tomfoolery, in imitation of certain sacred rites of our holy religion.

Lawyer, n. One skilled in circumvention of the law.

Life, n. A spiritual pickle preserving the body from decay.

Man, n. An animal so lost in rapturous contemplation of what he thinks he is as to overlook what he indubitably ought to be. His chief occuption is extermination of other animals and his own species, which, however, multiplies with such insistent rapidity as to infest the whole habitable earth and Canada.

Non-Combatant, n. A dead Quaker.

Omen, n. A sign that something will happen if nothing happens.

Once, adv. Enough.

Optimist, n. A proponent of the doctrine that black is white.

When bierce tired

of the routine at his editorial desk he would resort to the journalistic technique so well learned during his London years: pub crawling. San Francisco's challenging cocktail route began at the Baldwin Theater bar at Kearny and Bush, took in a half-dozen watering holes along Kearny to Market including the magnificent saloon at Hacquette's and Hageman's Crystal Palace, and finally wound its way to Market and Powell. Bierce's consumption of alcohol was truly amazing. He would usually drink twice as much as his favorite companions on these outings, Arthur McEwen and Petey Bigelow of the *Examiner*, and end up escorting them safely home. McEwen eventually grew to be such a fervent admirer of Bierce's capacity for liquor and his ability to write brilliantly the following day as to decide that the initials preceding his surname on the byline of the column – A. G. – stood for Almighty God. Everyone in the city, including the Prattler himself, appreciated the well-intentioned wit behind McEwen's proclamation. For Bierce (whose definition of *christen* was "to ceremoniously afflict a helpless child with a name"), the title of Almighty God was far more welcome than Ambrose Gwinett, the first and middle names he'd been given.

But all was not lighthearted fun and games during these early years at the *Wasp*. After having virtually destroyed the dangerous political career of Denis Kearney the Prattler turned his full attention to an even more powerful foe in the Big Four. Bierce had been a longtime opponent of these greedy and unbelievably ruthless railroad tycoons who all but owned California after the financial collapse of the seventies, and now he was working for a paper that openly supported his antirailroad viewpoint. His quarter-century feud with one of the most powerful and corrupt political forces in America began in earnest shortly after the infamous Battle of Mussel Slough – one of the most flagrantly unjust and reprehensible episodes in the history of this country.

Although the battle occurred in May of 1880, Bierce did not learn the facts behind the horrendous event until after his return from the Black Hills. It seemed that during the 1870s the kingpins of the Southern Pacific ran one of their railroad lines through California's San Joaquin Valley, and the executives, anxious to populate the region, advertised widely throughout the East about the fertile land of this area, which was being offered at extremely low prices. The result was that many settlers from the East as well as the Mid-West, seeking a better life and more freedom, were attracted to the Big Valley of California. Not wishing to take immediate title to the real estate for tax reasons, the Big Four relied on the naiveté of the settlers to accept a "gentlemen's agreement" whereby the railroad would offer them the land at an average price of $2.50 to $5.00 per acre as soon as the company perfected its title to the government land. In the meantime the settlers leased the land, gradually began making improvements and irrigated the arid soil until it was transformed into highly productive land. However, when the Big Four finally announced that it had taken title to the land in 1879 it formally issued its terms for sale of the property to the settlers at $25 to $35 an acre, with all the land to be sold on the open market to the highest bidder. Quickly pointing out the injustice of the entire matter, the settlers took their case through the appropriate legal channels and ended up in the U.S. Supreme Court. In the meantime the Big Four decided not to wait for the wheels of the judicial process to begin turning and on their own began moving new settlers upon the disputed land. When this happened the original settlers banded together and burned two of the newcomers' houses as a warning to the others. In retaliation the railroad secured eviction notices for several of the original settlers in favor of two supposed purchasers. And these two, who were in fact hired gunfighters, together with a U.S. marshal and a railroad land agent arrived at the settlement of Mussel Slough near the town of Hanford to formally evict the defiant settlers. When a group of armed settlers intercepted them at the Henry Brewer Ranch, gunfire broke out and resulted in the death of five of the settlers and both of the hired gunmen.

Under indictment for resisting a federal officer, seven of the settlers were arrested and stood trial in San Francisco. Eventually five of them were convicted and sentenced to eight months in a San Jose jail. In the eyes of the many antirailroad Californians the settlers were martyrs, and after they had served their terms three thousand supporters assembled to welcome them back to their homes. It was a victory of sorts, for until that time no one had ever seriously stood up against the tyrannical business manipulations of the all-powerful Big Four.

The murders at Mussel Slough would be immortalized some twenty years later in Frank Norris's 1901 novel *The Octopus*. This was a brilliant social drama of unprecedented proportions in American literature, but *The Octopus* was written with the luxury of a two-decade perspective on the monopolistic Southern Pacific and the tragic incident at Mussel Slough. Although the novel was quickly adopted by the antirailroad forces upon its publication at the turn of the century, Bierce was the only man in the entire country with the courage and the talent to launch an effective journalistic attack on the Big Four monopoly when it was at the height of its powers, during the eighties and nineties.

In his "Prattle" columns the political and economic octopus that was the Southern Pacific was hacked apart, tentacle by tentacle, with the sharp edge of Bierce's sardonic wit. He pointed to the "railrogues" as living proof of how insolent capitalism can lead to graft, bribes and outright intimidation of the public. When publicity men designated some of the trains "flyers" Bierce howled that these were no different than their other trains, and added that ticket holders on the Southern Pacific were riding the slowest trains in the country . . . trains invariably so late that passengers were actually "exposed to the perils of senility" before arriving at their destinations.

When the brass at the Southern Pacific protested about Bierce's harsh words he ran for the salt to pour into their wounds. He warned his readers that buying one of their tickets was like entering a suicide lottery, and for years he took pleasure in listing "the methods devised by the railroad company to punish the Demon Passenger." A typical aside in 1882 read: "The Overland arrived at midnight last night, more than nine hours late, and twenty passengers descended from the snow-covered cars. All were frozen and half-starved, but thankful they had escaped with their lives."

Bierce's sights were ultimately set on the men behind the trains and their corrupt business and political dealings. He attacked them as a gang of knaves and for twenty years chided the public for not seeing that the state and national legislators were bribed, slaves to the demands of their corporation overlords. He protested tirelessly against "the freebooters of the Railroad" and announced "we believe these men to be public enemies and indictable criminals. We believe that their wealth, illegally acquired, is sinfully enjoyed and will be dishonestly transmitted." In referring to Leland Stanford in print he would either call him "Stealand Landford" or "£eland $tanford," and Collis P. Huntington, as president of the Southern Pacific, came under heavy fire in most of the columns. Within a few years Bierce's belief that all men are hopeless rogues was further justified, in his estimation, when Stanford decided to run for the U.S. Senate and faced a candidate named Aaron Sargent, who, as it happened, was supported by Huntington. After Stanford was voted into office the two partners held a tremendous grudge against one another for what each man thought to be the other's defection. Bierce took advantage of the feud, and mercilessly played them against each other for years.

Despite Bierce's muckraking the railroad managed to keep its hold on the state of California, virtually owning both major political parties and most of the press. Indeed, Bierce was one of the few journalists who spoke out when a new Democratic-Republican coalition took over control of the state legislature but, with the members' pockets filled with Big Four bribe money, failed to get rid of Huntington's agents. When the new state legislature adjourned early after a particularly shameful session the Prattler took on more than railroad tycoons:

If nonsense were black, Sacramento would need gas lamps at noonday; if selfishness were audible, the most leather-lunged orator of the lot would appear a deaf mute flinging silly ideas from his finger tips amid the thunder of innumerable drums. So scurvy a crew I do not remember to have discovered in vermiculose conspiracy outside the carcass of a dead horse – at least not since they adjourned.

BIERCE'S HEALTH SUFFERED

as a result of warring with the railroad kings and taking on increasingly heavy editorial duties at the *Wasp* over a period of two years. His asthma was giving him more trouble than ever. In addition, although Bierce no longer welcomed Mollie's mother and brother, James, at the Bierce home in San Francisco, both Mrs. Day and her stuffy son often visited Mollie when Bierce was working, and soon Ambrose's total disgust with what he called the "Holy Trinity" became quite evident. It was obvious to him that they found strength in numbers and sided together against him on every conceivable subject. Bierce felt the only course left to him was to remove Mollie from their influence by packing his family off to remote Auburn (advertised as "the healthiest town in California"), and in 1883 he did so, giving hasty notice that he would surrender the active management of the *Wasp*. Undaunted by the move, which was as much to put distance between himself and the harsh Bay fogs as between Mollie and her family, Bierce continued his "Prattle" column without interruption. He filled his readers in on his new home in a little piece called "The Perverted Village":

> Sweet Auburn! liveliest village of the plain.
> Where Health and Slander welcome every train,
> Whence smiling innocence, its tribute paid,
> Retires in terror, wounded and dismayed –
> Dear lovely bowers of gossip and disease,
> Whose climate cures us that thy dames may tease,
> How often have I knelt upon thy green
> And prayed for death, to mitigate their spleen!

Of course, the problems between Ambrose and Mollie didn't disap-
pear. Their estrangement had been nurtured by in-law troubles for
over a decade, but to understand the real problem with the marriage
one must look to the egocentric and, even by Victorian standards,
total male chauvinism exhibited by Bierce. Like most men of that
time he lived by the convenient paradox of double-standard morality.
To a marriage a husband should bring "masculine experience"; a wife
nothing but her unquestioned virginity. However, it would verge on
paranoia to have women in particular single him out for his antifemi-
nist slander. He was every bit as hard on men and children. Bitter
Bierce was at war with mankind. That women were inferior beings,
weak and of low intelligence in his cynical world, was par for the
course. It's a simple fact that in his view 99 percent of all humanity
came out no better than a horse's ass. Bierce's journalistic assaults on
women are among the most sexist lines ever written – of this there is
no doubt – but the real point here is that he probably voiced the
opinions of the great majority of men during the Gilded Age, who
held the same attitudes but could not put them down on paper with
such unabashed vindictiveness. In the final analysis the major differ-
ence between the typical narrow-minded male chauvinist of the
1880s and Bierce was one of scope; he hated everyone equally.

Around this time Bierce's "Prattle" column began openly re-
flecting his deep pessimism about the institution of marriage. Soon
he was living like a hermit in a small room at Auburn's Putnam
House and would visit his family at his convenience. Mollie grew
increasingly disillusioned but tried to keep up the pretense of a successful marriage. It must have been hard with her husband now
openly flirting with other women, expecting clean children and hot
meals when he drunkenly bolted through the door at unexpected
hours and all the while busily adding definitions to "The Devil's Dictionary" such as the following:

Love, n. A temporary insanity curable by marriage.
Marriage, n. The state or condition of a community consisting of a
master, a mistress and two slaves, making in all, two.
Bride, n. A woman with a fine prospect of happiness behind her.
Husband, n. One who, having dined, is charged with the care of
the plate.

As a father Bierce could be extremely permissive one moment and
act like a dictator the next. His brooding moods could quickly cast a

dark cloud over an otherwise pleasant family gathering and cause his abrupt exit. He was a loner by nature and, in his relationship to his wife and three children, felt tied. Concerning the pride of fatherhood he wrote:

I don't believe that outside the heart of an insulate fool it ever existed. Why should it? – what is there to be proud of? It is a tradition of grannies and mid-wives, promoted by the vanity of girls and adopted by cackling bachelors as a catcall of derision.

Saddled with three children he should never have fathered, Bierce felt obligated to lay down some rules. First on the list was that they be well mannered and clean. Their father being one of the most fanatically neat and immaculately dressed gentlemen imaginable, it was unthinkable than any of his offspring be ill mannered or caught with dirty faces. He wanted the two boys in particular to be self-reliant and skeptical of everything they were taught in school. Once his oldest boy, Day, nervously reported to his father that he had slapped one of his teachers in the face after the teacher tried to punish him. Bierce not only applauded this independent and bold action but showed up at the school the following day with a menacing scowl and informed the teacher never to attempt such punishment again or he would show up packing more than a grimace. There were no more problems at school after that, and both boys grew up imitating their father in thought and behavior, learning to express themselves through writing with skill and wit while at the same time developing an absolute hatred of pretense.

Bierce gave of himself to Mollie and his children what he thought he could and, in return, asked them not to intrude too often on his privacy. One of the most amusing anecdotes of this period revolves around a minister's unexpected call on Mollie during one of her husband's visits. As it happened Leigh, the younger boy, ran into the parlor to report, "Papa, Day just said 'Damn God.'"

With both Mollie and the visiting pastor flushed with embarrassment Ambrose calmly told his younger son, "Go and tell Day that I have repeatedly told him not to say 'Damn God' when he means 'God Damn.'"

By far the most alarming incident during Bierce's days on the *Wasp* was when he discovered that owner Charles Webb Howard was president of the Spring Valley Water Company. Having blasted the company in print as a "persistent public misdemeanant" for pestering the the city government of San Francisco for a raise in water rates every few months, the Prattler was told to take it easy on the company and gently informed as to the connection between it and owner Howard. Bierce flew into a terrible rage. The fact that Howard had been reaping a nice profit by having his water company buy up the majority of the advertising space the *Wasp* had sold since its inception made Bierce lash out at the owner himself. He promptly threatened to expose Howard in his own paper by writing a detailed article on how the owner had thereby siphoned company funds into his own pocket, unless he sold out immediately. When Howard tried to work out a compromise he was met by a wall of righteous resistance. "I was more obstinate than ever," Bierce later wrote about the incident, "and now when I remember the lofty scorn with which I greeted every overture of my employer, I am filled with admiration and convinced afresh that I was born to be Rear-Admiral of a trade union." Indeed, his "lofty scorn" resulted in Howard selling the *Wasp* to Edward C. Macfarlane to prevent an outright scandal. Who in the world of journalism but Bierce, as a mere columnist, could turn the tables so swiftly and virtually select the owner of his paper rather than the other way around?

From his foothill retreat Bierce would mail in his column every week, continuing to delight his growing readership by debunking everything and everyone he felt worthy of his venom. Missionaries were described as "men who would beat a dog with a crucifix." A French journalist came under fire as "suffering from an unhealed wound . . . . his mouth." And, of course, there was the book review that, in its merciless brevity, very likely created nightmares for legions of aspiring novelists: "The covers of this book are too far apart."

By this time Bierce had attained the position of West Coast dean of literature. Those young writers who were not too intimidated by his reputation sometimes sought him out in Auburn and were usually surprised to find a thoroughly charming man. While his writings often suggested a tormented soul, these writers found Bierce quite open and willing to share his views on literature as well as evaluate their work. Writers he found promising but lacking in knowledge of a certain area he would take under his wing like a private tutor, suggesting reading lists that emphasized the classics. Doubtless his great ego thrived on these meetings where his admirers literally sat at his feet to catch droplets of wisdom. Sadly, he

took no such time with his own family. He could spend hours hypno-
tizing a perfect stranger with his personality and vast knowledge of
literature, but when it came to his own flesh and blood he would feel
they were wasting his time.

Late in 1885 the new owner of the *Wasp*, Edward C. Macfarlane, found himself in ill health and simply not suited to the
pressure-filled job of running a newspaper. He sold out to Col. J. P.
Jackson of the *Evening Post* and Bierce remained on the staff until the
spring of the following year, when his last column appeared and he
split with the *Wasp* forever.

At the age of

forty-three a restless and unemployed Ambrose Bierce moved his
family to the charming little town of Saint Helena on the advice of a

WHEN THE BIERCE FAMILY MOVED INTO THEIR NEW HOME
IN SAINT HELENA IN 1886, AMBROSE WAS AT BEST A
WEEKEND VISITOR, BUT IT WAS HERE THAT BIERCE
LAUNCHED HIS CAREER AS A FICTION WRITER.

friend who was convinced that the dry mountain climate would cure his asthma within a year. Situated at the north end of the beautiful Napa Valley, the town was well known as a health resort, but Bierce's chief concern was housing his family in the town proper and then finding employment. The first problem was remedied when an old San Francisco friend, a Captain Grant, offered his house on Main Street in Saint Helena and the Bierces gratefully accepted. Settling in the house (which is now a bed and breakfast inn, "The Ambrose Bierce House") was one hurdle crossed, but getting back into journalism would be quite another thing. Although he had built a tremendous readership as the Prattler over the years he had also managed to infuriate newspaper publishers across the country. The word was out that he could not be trusted and would bite the hand that fed him. When he wrote that journalism was "conducted by rogues and dunces for dunces and rogues" most publishers winced and gave second thought to hiring such an unpredictable sort. The enemies he had made were coming back to haunt him. Bitter Bierce had become too much of a high-risk stock to invest in.

Once Mollie and the children were comfortably settled into the Saint Helena house Bierce again absented himself from normal family life. This time he took up residence at a tiny health resort known as Angwin's Camp some seven miles away, situated on Howell Mountain. Irony of ironies, this same land where Bierce sought refuge would later become the settlement of Angwin and home of the Pacific Union College and the Saint Helena Hospital and Health Center—both staunch Seventh Day Adventist institutions. The old atheist is probably rolling over in his grave after this most paradoxical turn of events. Regardless, at the time Angwin's Camp, ideally set high among the pines, must have been soothing to his asthmatic condition as well as his still-undomesticated nature. Weekends were usually spent back at the house in Saint Helena with the family, where daughter Helen remembered him being moody and silent most of the time; a figure around whom the entire family had to walk on tiptoes. In an article written by Helen many years later entitled "Ambrose Bierce at Home" she recalled that even during these weekend visits her father "brooded by himself most of the time, sitting motionless and wordless by the library fire."

This division of time brings the observer back to the apparent dual personality Bierce embodied. As a family man he was a disaster, sullen and distant most of the time. Yet as a public figure he could be wonderfully engaging and full of life when he chose to be so, especially around the female members of his growing army of literary disciples. He was relatively unselfish with his time and criticism when young women writers such as Emma Dawson, Madge Morris and Ella Sterling Cummins showed up at his door with their manuscripts in hand.

In these early days in the Napa Valley Bierce's most famous liaison was a nonliterary coupling with the legendary Lillie Coit. At that time the flamboyant honorary member of the Knickerbocker Fire Engine Company No. 5 of San Francisco was separated from her husband and spending a good deal of time on her Larkmead estate called "Lonely," north of town. An early-emancipated woman who outraged Nob Hill society, the blond and busty "Firebelle Lillie" must have shocked Saint Helena residents to their countrified bones when she rode into town with her four-horse team wearing short skirts and hunting boots. Before long she found herself visiting Bierce at his retreat, and the two of them would often traipse off together and go hunting or hiking in the woods all day. There were also wild and scandalous house parties at Lonely where all the guests were men. You couldn't find a more brash or uninhibited female than Lillie Coit, yet Bierce's constant attacks on woman's suffrage and his iron-clad ideas as to how a proper lady should conduct herself were not applied in her case. "Lil Coit," he once told a friend, "is a real woman."

4
THE PRATTLER
VERSUS
THE WORLD

AMBROSE BIERCE'S YEAR
in exile from the world of journalism on Howell Mountain was a rejuvenating experience. Everything seemed to slow down in the dry
and sunny climate of the wine country. Now he had time to pursue
his favorite hobbies: collecting arrowheads, bicycling, gathering pine
cones and visiting old Schram's winery at the north end of the valley.
These were sleepy, carefree days which saw Bierce making pine-
needle pillows for his friends and taking his daughter into the woods
to listen to the songs of birds that, according to Helen, "gathered in
clouds upon his outstretched arms and head." His uncanny rapport
with all wild animals has been chronicled by several of his
biographers and by all accounts seems to be a truly mystic union.
But just when you're ready to forgive the great curmudgeon and
accept him as an animal lover with a heart of gold he turns the tables
and professes his intense hatred of dogs: "Smilers and defilers,
reekers and leekers."

Toward the end of 1886 Bierce decided to take up residence at a
modest apartment in Oakland in order to make some business contacts, while his family remained in Saint Helena. In March of the following year a young William Randolph Hearst (after being dis-

missed from Harvard when he presented chamberpots to various members of the faculty) took over control of his father's paper, the San Francisco *Examiner*. Actually the newspaper was a present from George Hearst to his twenty-three-year-old son in celebration of the elder Hearst's new duties as a California senator. With a healthy circulation of 30,000 the *Examiner* was the strongest Democratic daily paper in the state. However, while William Randolph agreed with his father's policy of opposition to the Southern Pacific he thought the paper itself could be more innovative and colorful. "We must be alarmingly enterprising," Hearst is quoted in the biography by Older as having written to his father, "and we must be startlingly original. We must be honest and fearless."

At that time the word *fearless* was synonymous with Ambrose Bierce, and Hearst knew it. He realized that hiring reporters and editorial writers who stirred up controversy was of the utmost importance in boosting circulation, and he decided to start at the top by sailing across the Bay to Oakland to approach the famous satirist. Bierce himself described his first meeting with Hearst many years later in his *Collected Works* by explaining that he was awakened from a midday nap by a gentle tapping at his door:

I found a young man, the youngest man, it seemed to me, that I had ever confronted. His appearance, his attitude, his manner, his entire personality suggested extreme diffidence. I did not ask him in, install him in my better chair (I had two) and inquire how we could serve each other. If my memory is not at fault I merely said, "Well" and awaited the result.

"I am from the San Francisco Examiner," he explained in a voice like the fragrance of violets made audible, and backed a little away.

"Oh," I said, "you come from Mr. Hearst." Then that unearthly child lifted its blue eyes and cooed: "I am Mr. Hearst."

Regardless of the fact that Bierce was twice the age of his future employer, the two men managed to come to terms. Hearst's overemphasis on a generous salary was counterbalanced by Bierce's indifference to money matters; his primary interest was in reviving the "Prattle" column without editorial revisions and that he be accorded a weekly byline on the editorial page. When Hearst agreed to these conditions he virtually gave free rein to Bierce and hence unleashed one of the first truly independent columnists in the history of journalism.

Throughout their twenty-year association both men were keenly aware that they were using each other. Bierce needed the money and a forum for his ideas, Hearst needed a strong circulation-building columnist. Bierce was permitted to live where he pleased and had no real connection with the reporting staff. All Hearst insisted on was that he receive the handwritten copy each week by mail for the next edition.

Bierce's first column appeared on March 27, 1887, and it was this Sunday issue that marked the beginning of his rocky two-decade link with the *Examiner*. Soon he was back to lampooning everything from naval design and local poets to worldwide politics and society in general. With the help of talented journalists like Arthur McEwen and Petey Bigelow, already on the staff, the *Examiner's* circulation greatly increased, and it soon became the first eight-page daily in San Francisco. Unknown to publisher Hearst, McEwen and Bigelow were also Bierce's treasured drinking buddies from his days on the *Wasp* and the old group formed such a fearsome trio on the cocktail route that they were often pointed out as a strange kind of tourist attraction. It seems Bigelow might have slightly overestimated his alcoholic tolerance, for one day at the office, caught in severe writer's block, he announced to no one in particular, "there are two things I'm going to do right now—have a glass of beer and go to France." With that he threw down his pen and dramatically stormed out of the editorial offices . . . only to return a year later and sit down at his desk as if he'd been down the street for a two-hour business lunch.

After he closed the deal with the *Examiner* Bierce returned to Saint Helena for a few days to visit with his family, and then made his way back up to his mountain retreat. He must have been in good spirits after having had such a well-paid job dumped in his lap. In later years he would write that he joined the Hearst forces because of "the easy nature of the service"—and perhaps a single "Prattle" column per week did seem easy after performing truly gargantuan editorial duties in all his previous newspaper work in addition to producing his column. With this extra time on his hands he began experimenting with the short story. For the previous few years visions of his Civil War days had fallen into a sharper focus and consumed his thoughts. Twenty-five years had passed since the battle of Shiloh, yet through his obsession with the horrors of war Bierce saw it more clearly than ever. He decided to devote his spare time to writing short fiction using the Civil War as a background, and the first tangible result of this effort, entitled "One of the Missing," was published in the *Examiner* early in 1888. Although the story itself was written in a somewhat formal, almost journalistic style, it is this reserved "military" tone that hypnotizes the reader. It was a very different kind of war story for the period, devoid of patriotic sentiment and glorious descriptions of proud young men marching off to battle. In a chillingly impersonal style Bierce educated his reader about the true nature of war: the effects of fear, the nauseating sense of foreboding and the seemingly absurd coincidences that are, in reality, a part of every battle. At forty-six years old Ambrose Bierce had entered the world of fiction, and over the next few years his growing collection of

THIS MACABRE PORTRAIT OF BIERCE WAS EXHIBITED AT THE WORLD'S FAIR IN 1893, WHERE IT WON A GOLD MEDAL.

war stories would attract a great deal of attention. They would finally bring him national fame, which had eluded him for so many years.

Living a life of semiseclusion on Howell Mountain, Bierce's more unconventional character traits became even more pronounced. Writing by candlelight from midnight to dawn with a human skull on his desk (possibly a source of inspiration for some of his early efforts in writing horror stories), he also maintained a small menagerie, consisting of several frogs, snakes, tame squirrels, birds and a large lizard that he sometimes kept perched on his shoulder while he wrote. His eccentric behavior was not confined to the privacy of his mountain hideaway, either. Increasingly, when he ventured out into the town of Saint Helena or journeyed south to San Francisco, he refused to speak or shake hands with former friends who had disappointed him in one way or another. Another odd habit was his formally "disintroducing" himself from casual business acquaintances who had had the misfortune of turning into professional enemies, which usually left the unsuspecting foe speechless and completely baffled.

Bierce's role as an absentee husband and father was finally wearing thin. In his opinion things were just fine as they were—he was free to travel where he pleased, meet interesting people in the arts and give tender counsel to his female protégés while, at the same time, knowing that the door to a loving wife and three children was always open to him in Saint Helena. The one-sided nature of this arrangement would never have occurred to Bierce, a truly classic case in the annals of male chauvinism. Mollie, however, began seriously questioning their relationship and reminiscing about the carefree days before her marriage, when she was happy and had more than her share of admirers. Even now, with teenage children, she was very attractive and impressed the citizens of Saint Helena as an outgoing and thoroughly captivating woman. She had impeccable social graces, ran a household single-handedly, and was an avid gardener and a talented pianist. To understand what she was up against one must imagine her opening the Sunday *Examiner* in the serene morning sun bathing the Napa Valley and then turning to the "Prattle" column and reading her husband's comment that "a bad marriage is like an electric thrilling-machine: it makes you dance, but you can't let go."

Between her husband's long absences from Saint Helena and

his public attacks on the institution of marriage, Mollie quite understandably needed to be reassured that she was desirable to the opposite sex. The confirmation that she was indeed an attractive woman came from a wealthy Danish bachelor who was accustomed to spending his summers in the town and found her totally irresistible. Although it was a completely innocent flirtation on her part it lasted the entire season, and Mollie was undeniably pleased by the attention. Soon the Dane's intentions went beyond the point of flirtation; when he pleaded with Mollie to leave her husband she adamantly refused to consider it. However, there was a strong attraction between them, and she received some passionate love letters after he left Saint Helena. As fate would have it Ambrose found one of the letters during one of his infrequent visits and flew into a rage. In a magazine article published years later Helen Bierce wrote:

There was a big scene when he found the Dane's letter and after that he packed his things and left, never to return. Mother was broken-hearted. She did not see the other man again, and she swore to me that it had not been a real romance, but Father would not listen – it was enough that she had permitted some love-letters to be written to her.

Later in that same article the only daughter born of that ill-starred union summed up her father's tragic misunderstanding of, and antiquated attitude toward, womanhood:

I believe it was his lack of understanding, of sympathy, of appreciation for women that caused the trouble. He was the soul of sincerity in all he wrote, but I feel somehow that with women it was different. He expected too little of them mentally. He had the ancients' view of them as chattels, demanding of them fidelity and service, but it never occurred to him to think with them.

"I don't take part in competitions – not even in love," wrote Bierce to a friend shortly after his separation from Mollie. His fierce pride and ultrasensitive ego simply could not accept what had happened, however innocent it might have been. His wife had broken her master's rules. She had entertained the admiration of another man and would now pay the price. There was no room for discussion. Sixteen years of a one-sided marriage had finally come to an abrupt end. Bierce moved away to Sunol, completely disheartened yet stubbornly refusing to listen to Mollie's pleadings that the entire episode was a misunderstanding.

AFTER MOVING INTO A

modest hotel in Sunol Bierce decided that the best method of taking his mind off the separation was to bury himself in his work. His "Prattle" columns were on the increase, and although he usually mailed in his material, Bierce was often compelled to travel to the *Examiner* office in San Francisco to iron out editorial problems. During the course of these visits he gradually became aware of William Randolph Hearst's increasingly complex personality. Their early contact had been comically superficial, but the old cynic had been eyeing Hearst for several months with an increased sense of puzzlement as well as respect. The boy publisher was finding his legs, so to speak, and was quickly developing into quite a character himself. To Bierce's complete astonishment Hearst, after having caught one of the managerial men red-handed stealing *Examiner* money, kept the man on at the same position and later explained: "I have a new understanding with him. He is to steal only small sums hereafter; the largest are to come to me."

There was a very human and unconventional side to the young Hearst that Bierce found most attractive. He would often emerge from his office without notice and execute an Irish jig for the enjoyment of the hard-nosed newsmen in the editorial room, then calmly return to his duties as publisher. During these early days in their professional relationship he won Bierce's respect simply by being unpredictable. When one of the *Examiner's* editors was offered an outright bribe by an official of the Spring Valley Water Company, the editor kicked the company man out of his office with self-righteous glee, exhilarated in the pride so apparent in a man who refuses to be corrupted. When young Hearst heard about the episode, he flew into a rage: "You're a fool," he yelled at his editor. "Why didn't you take the money and keep up the fight just the same? He would never have dared to say a word about it."

The mutual-admiration society formed between Bitter Bierce and Hearst during these early years at the *Examiner* was a mystery to almost everyone in journalism. They were both very powerful and controversial men, yet their egos did not clash. Bierce, being the creative force, was always given the benefit of the doubt by his employer, who had read and admired the cynic's column during his stormy college days. Though Bierce was old enough to be Hearst's father, it was Hearst who defended his star columnist's excesses with paternal passion in every altercation, however trifling. A case in point was Bierce's criticism of the product of famed California vintner Arpad Haraszthy in his "Prattle" column:

The wine of Arpad Haraszthy has a bouquet all its own. It tickles and tit-illates the palate. It gurgles as it slips down the alimentary canal. It warms the cockles of the heart, and it burns the sensitive lining of the stomach.

Haraszthy was outraged by the column and immediately consulted his lawyers and demanded that they threaten the *Examiner* with a lawsuit unless Bierce ran a retraction. Bierce and Hearst were equally insulted by the threats of libel issued by the vintner, and the "retraction" in the next column was a good example of how the writer and publisher could team to jointly thumb their noses at legal threats as well as deliver a highly sarcastic apology:

The wine of Arpad Haraszthy does not have a bouquet all its own. It does not tickle and titillate the palate. It does not gurgle as it slips down the alimentary canal. It does not warm the cockles of the heart, and it does not burn the sensitive lining of the stomach.

"Prattle," successful in its two previous vehicles, was in the *Exam-iner* again the most eagerly read column of causerie printed in Ameri-ca, and it boosted newspaper sales by annihilating political and liter-ary enemies each in single blows. Bierce's savagery in print was so furious that Franklin K. Lane, later secretary of the interior, labeled him "an outlaw from the human species" and added that the satirist was "a hideous monster so like a mixture of dragon, lizard, bird and snake as to be unnameable."

As in the past, Bierce was forever eager to explain the differ-ence between wit and humor to his readers:

In a matter of this kind it is easier to illustrate than to define. Humor (which is not inconsistent with pathos, so nearly allied are laughter and tears) is Charles Dickens; wit is Alexander Pope. Humor is Dogberry; wit is Mercutio . . . nearly all Americans are humorous; if any are born witty, heaven help them to emigrate! You shall not meet an American and talk with him two minutes but he will say something humorous; in ten days he will say nothing witty; and if he did, your own, O most witty of all possible readers, would be the only ear that would give it recognition. Humor is tolerant, tender; its ridicule caresses. Wit stabs, begs par-don – and turns the weapon in the wound. Humor is a sweet wine, wit a dry; we know which is preferred by the connoisseur.

By This Time

the well-known bitterness exhibited by Bierce in his column was reaching new heights. His failed marriage, and therefore the institution of marriage in general, he now linked to his exceedingly pessimistic view of society. In November of 1888 he wrote:

Marriage being a human institution, is a failure. It is no more or less a failure than religion, philosophy, science, art, literature, law, medicine, government, or any other large affair capable of conception as a means to a desirable end. The entire scheme of "civilization and enlightenment" is a failure of the most lamentable sort.

Another failure of "the most lamentable sort" was taking shape a hundred miles to the north, where his eldest son Day had been working as reporter on the Red Bluff *Sentinel*. It seems that young Day had inherited his father's confidence, artistic temperament, sensitivity and journalistic leanings to the degree that he left the safety of his Saint Helena home to seek his destiny in the world of journalism at the age of fifteen. Despite strong protests from his mother and father, Day stubbornly stuck to his decision and chose to make it on his own. He was said to have been exceedingly good looking and a remarkably accomplished writer for such a tender age, yet plagued by the same sense of pride that so affected his father—a blind pride so powerful that it prevented him from accepting a modest sum of money sent to him by his mother and prompted a curt letter of total disdain and the immediate return of the money.

It also seems that young Day had adopted his father's attitudes toward courtship and women. At the age of sixteen, already an established reporter in Red Bluff, he cut a striking figure as a blond Adonis who had an eye for the ladies. In April of 1889, while covering a lodge picnic in the neighboring town of Chico, Day was strongly attracted to a girl his own age named Eva Adkins, a voluptuous and flirtatious girl who worked in a cannery nearby. Day was so captivated by the girl's beauty that he resigned his post on the *Sentinel* and, in his youthful exuberance, moved to Chico and found a job in the cannery just to be near her.

While Day's impetuous infatuation with the comely Eva turned into a one-sided love affair, she set her sights elsewhere. Through Day, ironically, Eva had met another youth by the name of Neil Hubbs; this innocent introduction was soon to be the basis of a tragic romantic triangle, for as it turned out Eva became more interested in Hubbs. In the meantime Day, feeling he had a special hold on the fascinating Eva, moved into the boarding home run by her mother. He kept such close tabs on her as to have knocked out a drunk who insulted her on the street, and jealously guarded her reputation when she took a job as a maid at the Tilton House by making sure she did not speak to the boarders.

Like father, like son—Day Bierce went around with a gun on his hip that was as quick as his temper. Although he and Eva were only sixteen, Day insisted that they be engaged. Eva agreed in order to pacify the insistent Day but seemingly put an end to the problem by slipping out of town two days before the proposed wedding to elope with Hubbs. After their marriage in French Camp the newlyweds returned to Eva's mother's house in Chico. Upon their arrival Day confronted the couple in the living room in a most cordial and aloof manner and then disappeared into his bedroom upstairs. Apparently Hubbs had caught wind of the conflict whirling within the soul of his tormented friend and drew his revolver, keeping it at the ready by his side. Suddenly an insanely jealous Day flung open the door of his upstairs bedroom and ran down the stairs firing.

By all accounts both men fired simultaneously, but Day's shots were by far the more accurate. One of his shots hit Hubbs, who scrambled out the door. Then the irate lover fired at his intended, aiming at her head but only grazing her ear. At this point Hubbs, hearing his wife's screams, ran back into the house and wrestled the gun from the hysterical Day. "My God, Neil," Day screamed after seeing the blood on the floor, "what have I done? Just put a cartridge in your revolver and kill me . . . . I'm not fit to live."

Hubb's thoughts were not on revenge as much as getting his bride to a doctor. The newlyweds fled the house, and Day, in his insane grief over what had occurred, made his way back upstairs, laid a chloroform-soaked cloth over his face and fired a shot from his own pistol into his right temple.

"Horrible! Horrible!" screamed the headlines of the Chico *Enterprise* the following day. "Bierce will die, with one chance in ten for Hubbs."

As it turned out both Day Bierce and Neil Hubbs were mortally wounded and died within a few hours of each other on July 27, 1889. According to the Chico newspaper a "sadly broken" Ambrose Bierce traveled north from Oakland to claim his son's body. When he came face to face with his departed firstborn on a marble slab at the undertaker's he commented soberly, "You are a noble soul, Day. You did just right."

Later that day Bierce started out for Saint Helena with his son's body. Several days later he would bury Day in an unmarked grave and set his eyes on his estranged wife for the last time at the funeral services. For several weeks he would carry Day's ivory-handled revolver around with him. Then, finally, he would throw it away, and wonder whether the bleak outlook that was so prevalent in his past writings had somehow cast a dark shadow over his future.

5
At the feet
of the
master

Shortly after day's

death Bierce took up residence at the Sunol Glen Hotel in Sunol, California. The proprietors of the modest country hotel were honored by the presence of the famed journalist and greatly pleased by the increase in business generated by his loyal flock of admirers. His hosts were also burdened with nursing him through several severe attacks of asthma, as well as depressions about his separation and his oldest son's suicide, which rendered him speechless for several days at a time other than his repetition of one pitiful phrase – "nothing matters."

He did, however, weather the storm, and during the following years his renowned crustiness took a second seat to a superhuman surge of creative energy. His dark moods finally found a worthy outlet in his fiction, and his short stories began piling up. In the meantime his work in "Prattle" continued to be amusingly cynical and lashed out at anyone and anything that came to mind. As uninhibited as ever with his criticism and moral rantings, Bierce's ego wasn't so inflated that he refused minor editorial supervison, but his touchy nature was such that whenever he felt his column was excessively blue-penciled he would resign in a fiery rage. Since a formal resignation signed by the Prattler himself made its way to Hearst's desk once or twice a year, the young publisher learned to stay on the good side of the temperamental columnist by supporting him in all major altercations with the editors. Hearst even traveled to Sunol to placate his star writer on several occasions and personally urged him to stay on at the *Examiner* after the stubborn columnist had waged a particularly bitter fight against editors whom he described as "half wits who pick the meat out of my stew."

During Bierce's stay in Sunol one of many female admirers who came to call on him was the talented novelist Gertrude Atherton.

Ambrose Bierce

Young, blonde and shapely, the recently widowed Mrs. Atherton asked him if he could look over one of her manuscripts for any criticism or comments. Bierce felt he could surely make room for another saucy protégé in his select group of women admirers. In her autobiography, *Adventures of a Novelist,* Atherton admitted she was "consumed by curiosity" and then related the following story of their ill-fated, comically awkward encounter:

Bierce was about forty-nine at the time, a tall man, very thin and closely knit, with curly iron gray hair, a bristling moustache, beetling brows over frowning eyes, good features and beautiful hands. His appearance did not appeal to me, however, for he looked too much like my father – what my mother would have called a typical Yank. We eyed each other rather oppugnantly when he met me at the train. I was by way of giving him to understand that although I admired his work, and had gone out of my way to meet him, I had no intention of falling down and worshipping him. What was in his own mind I never knew. I had on a very becoming blue frock, and presumably he thought I was vain and spoilt and a member of the idle rich who wrote merely to amuse herself.

The luncheon passed off well enough in that dreary fly-specked dining-room; S. S. Chamberlain, the editor of the "Examiner," was present and he was an easy and brilliant talker. But he disappeared when the meal was over – and Bierce led me into his bedroom! He looked cynical and somewhat amused.

I did not turn a hair, however, and settled myself in the one comfortable chair, while he, with a muttered apology, lay down on the bed! Invalids have their privileges.

It was the most disagreeable afternoon I ever spent. We quarrelled incessantly. On every conceivable subject. He tore my books to rags. I had promise, but I had written nothing as yet worthy of serious consideration. This might be true, but I wasn't going to admit it to him, and I retaliated by criticizing his own work. His stories might be models of craftsmanship and style, and he had mastered the technique of horror, but they were so devoid of humanity that they fell short of true art, and would never make any but a limited appeal. He congratulated me upon the mature judgment which no doubt had me in high demand as a critic.

We got round to authors in general. Meredith had been ignored for thirty years and should never have been "discovered" at all. Obscurity was the place for him. He could neither think straight nor write straight. His style was atrocious, and his characters as inchoate as his sentences. I was not enamoured of Meredith, but I defended him acidly. Never would I agree with that detestable man on any subject.

As for Stevenson, he was nothing but a phrase-maker; his imagination was so thin that it was all he could do to beat it out into a novel of conventional length. It was like an attenuated wire threatening to snap at any moment. No wonder he cultivated a style so artificial that it diverted what little discernment the average reader might possess from the pitiful lack of content. Novels were not worth writing anyway. The only form in which the perfection of art could be achieved, as well as the effect of totality, was that of the short story.

"The trouble with you," I said crudely, "is that you cannot write novels yourself. All short-story writers are jealous of novelists. They all try to write novels and few of them succeed. Any clever cultivated mind, with a modicum of talent, can manage the short story, even with no authentic gift for fiction – as you yourself have proved. But it takes a very special endowment and an abundant imagination to sustain the creative faculty throughout a story of novel length. To hold it up. Only the born novelist carries on without falling down over and over, stumbling along from one high spot to another."

And so it went. We almost spat at each other. And there would be no train until six o'clock!

Finally I thought I would change my tactics. After all the poor man was ill, and embittered through many misfortunes. He had lost his great opportunity when family obligations forced him to leave London. He was condemned to second-rate hotels in order to support an estranged wife and two children on his salary. And his eldest and favorite son – a boy of great promise – had recently been shot to death in a disgraceful fracas.

So I relented, told him I was sorry I had been so quarrelsome, for no one admired him more than I did. He was a great man and I was willing to admit it.

I might have saved myself the concession. He almost flew at me. He was not great. He wouldn't be called great. He was a failure, a mere hack. He got so red I feared he would have an attack of asthma. He gave me some twenty reasons why he wasn't great, but I have forgotten all of them. I still think him one of the greatest short-story writers that ever lived.

The shadows were lengthening. The short winter day was drawing to a close. I rose with a sigh of relief.

"A quarter to six," I said briskly. "And I'd like a breath of fresh air before two hours in that over-heated train."

As we walked to the station his manner changed. He became almost charming. He thanked me for coming to see him and apologized for being so cantankerous, said that he had found an irresistible pleasure in arguing with me, and that I was a blue and gold edition of all the poets!!!

The train was late. We walked about the station, conversing most amiably. It grew darker. We were in the shadows between the station and the malodorous grunting pigsty when he suddenly seized me in his

---

Ambrose Bierce

arms and tried to kiss me. In a flash I knew how to hurt him. Not by struggling and calling him names. I threw back my head – well out of his reach – and laughed gayly. "The great Bierce!" I cried. "Master of style! The god on Olympus at whose feet pilgrims come to worship – trying to kiss a woman by a pigsty!"

The train steamed in at the moment. He rushed me to it and almost flung me on board. "I never want to see you again!" he barked. "You are the most detestable little vixen I ever met in my life, and I've had a horrible day."

I smiled down at him from the platform. I knew my barb had gone in to the hilt, for women had spoilt him and no doubt he thought himself irresistible.

"I have only been mildly bored," I said sweetly. "And I certainly have too many pleasant places to visit to think of coming up here again to spend hours with a man in a chronic state of ill-temper."

During the following decades Atherton would attain a good deal of fame and money by writing popular novels like *A Daughter of the Vine,* which dealt with the sordid lives of prominent San Franciscans, and *Black Oxen,* which shocked the post–World War I generation with its frank treatment of sexual rejuvenation. Her novels were ahead of their time in that her heroines would often combine interesting careers, sexual freedom and independence. After assessing her own literary career and her courage in standing up to the much-feared Bierce it's probably safe to assume Gertrude Atherton knew of what she wrote.

In the Fall of 1891

Bierce's first book of fiction was published: *Tales of Soldiers and Civilians.* Although many of the short stories in this volume had appeared in the *Examiner* over a period of four years, from 1887 to 1891, they showed an amazing degree of continuity in both theme and tone. The nineteen tales of horror (almost evenly divided into two sections entitled "Soldiers" and "Civilians") were praised by the majority of critics as highly unique, novel and boldly experimental. The British edition, which appeared shortly thereafter, was published under the title *In the Midst of Life;* it omitted four of the stories printed in the American version and added nine from Bierce's earlier published work in newspapers. Most of the subsequent editions have followed the English table of contents as well as adopting the latter title.

Ambrose Bierce was the only writer of note to have served in the Civil War armies. His stories depicting the inhuman slaughter and insanity of battle serve as a rare firsthand record of undeniable historical importance. Although the war between the states produced four presidents, it allowed precious little literary talent to survive. However brilliant was Stephen Crane's *Red Badge of Courage* in its depiction of the war, it was written several years after *Tales of Soldiers and Civilians* by a man who was born six years after Lee surrendered at Appomattox. It was Bierce and Bierce alone who, according to H. L. Mencken, was "the first writer of fiction ever to treat war realistically," to tell us in no uncertain terms that soldiers are "bewildered animals dying like hogs in Chicago."

While there was no easy optimism in any of the stories in *Tales of Soldiers and Civilians,* those dealing with war were the darkest in mood. The Civil War was unquestionably the most significant factor contributing to the author's famed misanthropy. Bierce's feelings that soldiers were "hardened and impenitent man-killers" was chillingly advanced through the use of grisly black humor and macabre situations. His stories reflect the darker side of human nature in disturbingly honest terms—so disturbing, in fact, that brother Albert felt compelled to explain Ambrose's hauntingly bleak visions as symptoms of the head wound he received in the war. However. long before joining the army Bierce's morbid nature had been a source of concern to his family and friends. At the age of sixteen, for instance, he had had a nightmare that both God and mankind were dead, and decades later he incorporated the dream into a story called "Visions of the Night." Totally alone in the universe, he found himself walking into a room bathed in "the lawless light of dreams" and approached a bed.

Upon the bed, partly clothed, lay the dead body of a human being. It lay upon its back, the arms straight along the sides. By bending over it, which I did with loathing but no fear, I could see that it was dreadfully decomposed. The ribs protruded from the leathern flesh; through the skin of the sunken belly could be seen the protuberances of the spine. The face was black and shriveled and the lips, drawn away from yellow teeth, cursed it with a ghastly grin. A fullness under the closed lids seemed to indicate that the eyes had survived the general wreck; and this was true, for as I bent above them they slowly opened and gazed into mine with a tranquil, steady regard. Imagine my horror how you can—no words of mine can assist the conception; the eyes were my own! That vestigial fragment of a vanished race – that unspeakable thing which neither time nor eternity had wholly effaced – that hateful and abhorrent scrap of mortality, still sentient after the death of God and the angels, was I!

The psychological themes and bizarre blend of terror and black humor so evident in all of the tales in this first collection simply caught the Victorian reader off guard. It was a strikingly different book for the times, every story being shot through with bitter irony, and many – "Chickamauga," "A Horseman in the Sky," "An Occurrence at Owl Creek Bridge," "The Man and the Snake," "Killed at Resaca" and "A Watcher by the Dead," to name a few – became classics in the genre and have been widely reprinted over the past ninety years.

Bierce's reaction to any criticism of his stories was predictably irate. His sensitive ego was so easily bruised that he even resented some critics comparing him to Edgar Allen Poe, preferring to be thought of as an original and therefore incapable of being classified with any other writer. While his short fiction was unique and, in some cases, extremely innovative, today many of Bierce's tales seem melodramatic and old fashioned. Of course it should be remembered that they are nearing the century mark, and that they were written in an era when the literary mainstream considered the short story more of an intellectual exercise than an apt vehicle for talent on the order of Bierce's. Regardless, ever since the publication of *Tales of Soldiers and Civilians* modern critics have increasingly questioned the effectiveness of his stiff style, the "twist" endings to many of his stories and, above all, his two-dimensional characters. It was the lack of human compassion thereby expressed, the strange aloofness so evident in the author as well as in his fiction, that prompted Edmund Wilson to point out in his book *Patriotic Gore* how Bierce's obsession with death created a weak link in virtually all of his stories:

Death may perhaps be said to be Ambrose Bierce's only real character. In all Bierce's fiction, there are no men or women – that is, by reason of their passions, their aspirations or their personalities. They figure only as the helpless butts of sadistic practical jokes, and their higher faculties are so little involved that they might almost as well be trapped animals.

Indeed, Bierce's fiction is so devoid of human emotion and restricted by his failure to see the complexities of human behavior that most of his stories take on an odd, almost mythic quality, which relies on symbolic situations in a capsulated format. His theory that a novel is simply an easier way to write a short story was, by most estimations, an elaborate disguise for his literary deficiencies in the area of characterization. For whatever reason, Bierce's rejection of the novel as an art form was absolute, as evidenced by his definition in *The Devil's Dictionary* of the African tsetse fly as an insect "whose bite is commonly regarded as Nature's most efficacious remedy for insomnia, though some patients prefer that of the American novelist."

Bierce made his way back to familiar ground in November of 1891 when he again settled at Angwins Camp on Howell Mountain to find relief from his asthmatic condition. Early in the following year his first volume of poems, *Black Beetles in Amber,* appeared and caused quite a stir in San Francisco because of their literary lynching of many notables. However, most of the verse was collected from his newspaper columns and therefore much too localized to gain national attention. His keen wit and contempt were leveled against men no one now remembers. His targets were simply too small for his sizeable talents. After the war and horror stories from his first book made people across the country sit up and take notice, his *Black Beetles in Amber* was a move in the wrong direction, one critic understandably renaming it *Red Peppers in Vinegar.*

Around this time another strange literary episode was developing with the publication of *The Monk and the Hangman's Daughter,* a book still shrouded in mystery but originally represented as being coauthored by Bierce and his friend Dr. Adolphe Danziger. A dapper German immigrant, Dr. Danziger had been a dentist, a lawyer and a rabbi before joining the ranks of Bierce admirers and becoming one of his students. An aspiring poet and translator some twenty years younger than Bierce, Danziger's goal was to collaborate on a book with "der master." He was as enterprising as he was shrewd and quickly realized that he could capitalize on Bierce's gullibility and egocentric nature by praising his genius to the skies. It worked so well that early in their relationship Bierce defended Danziger from an attack in print by Dr. Jacob Voorsanger in the *Jewish Times and Observer* by writing in his column that "all the Voorsangers of all the synagogues might play leap-frog in the shadow of Danziger's mind." In fact the young writer followed his guru up to his retreat on Howell Mountain and rented a cottage nearby. Unfortunately, as recorded in the 1929 biography by Danziger (also known as Adolphe de Castro) entitled *Portrait of Ambrose Bierce,* "the fence-less harem of his feminine worshippers frequently annoyed me. But they adored him and came to bestow their affections on him without his permission. When I looked at him with 'brown envious eyes,' as he phrased it, he grinned, as the fox did when the raven dropped the baby rabbit."

After translating a long story called "Der Moench von Berch-tesgarden" by Richard Voss from the German, Danziger asked Bierce to polish the tale as a collaborator. Reluctant at first, Bierce was soon obsessed with editing and adding ironic twists to this odd psychological study of a man torn between sexual desire and relig-ious ecstasy, which ends in murder. It appeared initially as a serial in the *Examiner* in the fall of 1891 and the following year was published in book form as *The Monk and the Hangman's Daughter,* by the F. J. Schulte Company of Chicago. As it turned out Bierce and Danziger squabbled over the authorship of this story for years. The trouble began when Danziger protested at Bierce's name appearing before his on the title page. The furious Bierce was soon claiming that Dan-ziger was trying to snatch the larger share of proceeds from the book, and back and forth it went, each man belittling the other's contribu-tion to the book and claiming full authorship. In truth neither Danzi-ger's crude translation nor Bierce's minor stylistic improvements made the story that of either man alone; the theme, plot, and charac-terization were all from the pen of Richard Voss. It was Bierce who later realized that he and Danziger had been caught up in a petty lit-erary feud of little interest to anyone but themselves. He later wrote in a "Prattle" piece that it made absolutely no difference which of them had the largest share "in spoiling the work of a better man."

DURING THIS PERIOD

Bierce's residence alternated every few months between Angwin's Camp, Sunol and Oakland. On one of these trips he visited his brother Albert's camp on the shore of Lake Temescal in the hills behind Oakland and met a twenty-two-year-old poet named George Sterling. A Long Islander who came west in the early 1890s after re-jecting a career in the priesthood, Sterling had gone to work as a clerk in the Oakland real estate office of his uncle but soon found the business world an interminable bore. It was the Bohemian literary life around the Bay that really interested him, and soon he was haunting the restaurants and bars known to be frequented by the artists of the area. He had been an ardent admirer of Bierce's column in the Sunday *Examiner* for years. Their first meeting was agreed to by Bierce after he learned that before leaving Long Island Sterling and a friend had hoisted a pirate's flag on top of a church steeple. In Bierce's mind that was a sure indication of literary potential, and he was more than happy to look over a fellow atheist's work as well as to socialize and philosophize with the small group of other artists and writers present, who included painter J. H. E. Partington and an attractive woman reporter for the Oakland *Saturday Press* named Carroll Carrington. Sterling was so awed by Bierce that first night, he wrote about the meeting in his introduction to *The Letters of Ambrose Bierce,* entitled "A Memoir of Ambrose Bierce":

I am not likely to forget his first night among us. A tent being, for his ailment, insufficiently ventilated, he decided to sleep by the campfire, and I, carried away by my youthful hero-worship, must partially gratify it by occupying the side of the fire opposite to him. I had a comfortable cot in my tent, and was unaccustomed at the time to sleeping on the ground, the consequence being that I awoke at least every half-hour. But awake as often as I might, always I found Bierce lying on his back in the dim light of the embers, his gaze fixed on the stars of the zenith. I shall not forget the gaze of those eyes, the most piercingly blue, under shaggy brows, that I have ever seen.

Soon Sterling was calling Bierce "the master" and, in turn, quickly became one of the cynic's most serious and respected protégés. Just as in the Danziger episode, Bierce's ability to form an unbiased critical opinion of another writer who lauded his talents seemed hopelessly clouded. For the next twenty years Bierce claimed Sterling was a highly gifted artist whose work was the equal of any of the great nineteenth-century poets. Today, when the cream of Sterling's poetry can be considered good at best, it should also be remembered that in his last years Bierce was one of the first critics in the country to praise the work of another young poet – Ezra Pound.

Sterling was every bit as enthralled by the enigmatic Bierceian personality as was his court of lovely and adoring poetesses. When the master recommended a thorough reading of the classics Sterling followed his suggestions as if they were issued on a tablet and had appeared from the heavens on his doorstep. By the nineties Bierce's reputation was akin to that of a modern-day rock superstar. No writer's reputation was quite made in those days until Bierce officially pronounced him or her a genuine artist. But just as he could help a budding career like Sterling's with eloquent praise, with acid invective he could demolish one before it got off the ground, like that of David Lesser Lezinsky. While Bierce's attacks on the artistic incompetence of the young poet were no more brutal than those he had launched in earlier years, some critics cried foul and accused him of anti-Semitism. It is clear from his journalistic past that he had no qualms about attacking anyone, regardless of whether they belonged to one minority or another. It was his theory that taking it easy on anyone because of race or religion when the person was truly deserving of wrath would be no less a sin than practicing outright prejudice on the same basis. This was in fact an enlightened view, for anti-Semitism was at that time a socially and morally acceptable reaction of the WASP population against the period's surge of Jewish immigration. The uncompromising Bierce had his own set of ethical standards, and if he took on any group he would inevitably attack a majority, in order to insult as wide a range of individuals as possible. Tragically, Lezinsky committed suicide a few days after Bierce's comment that he was "suffering from excess emotionalism and should go to some asylum for a long rest." Rightly or not, the suicide seemed to unleash a minor reaction against Bierce's harsh methods of criticism. When he was blamed by some for the young poet's death he remained cool and objective. "It is perfect rot to say that I am responsible for Lezinsky's death," he told a friend. "I have never met him and would have refused to do so had the occasion risen. I never once attacked him personally but only his verse. When he elected to become a poet, he impliedly consented to public criticisms of that which he made public."

After the unfortunate fiasco of *The Monk and the Hangman's Daughter* Bierce partially redeemed his literary reputation with the publication in 1893 of his second book of short stories entitled *Can Such Things Be?* Of the twenty-five stories several masterpieces of his macabre art emerged, all revolving around the supernatural and the inherent humor found in horror. The book as a whole was rejected by many critics and readers simply because it was so chillingly morbid in tone. Even the questioning title of the book represents a certain challenge – are such things possible? . . . could this really happen? . . . *Can Such Things Be?*

Those not totally frightened off by the eerie tales witnessed a truly bizarre three-ring circus of ghosts and murders, animated machines and mad dogs, apparitions and extrasensory perceptions. Bierce's distaste for "marketing" a book to capture as wide an audience as possible was never more evident. During his lifetime his stories had a small but extremely devoted following that amounted to a literary cult. Although the cult has now grown into a large readership and much of his fiction has been anthologized in short-story collections and college texts, fallacious criticism (a favorite and often quoted line about his tales labeled them "Poe plus sulphur") has damaged the reputation of his work. Nevertheless, today Bierce is the recognized master of two specialized fields: the murder story as black humor and the sardonic ghost story.

The stories in *Can Such Things Be?* displayed significant psychological insight and explored the realm of fear as few others had before them. Bierce's mastery of the "outré," the unusual, went unquestioned. In his bloodcurdling tales of murder and freak accidents he ingeniously convinced the reader that death is a joke. In the farce called life, death was elevated to high comedy. Alienation and a keen sense of the absurd are present in nearly every story. There are children who murder their parents, dead men who refuse to stay buried and sons who seduce their mothers, all ghoulishly told with shockingly ironic twists and unsettling humor.

A few of the tales worth singling out for their innovation are "Moxon's Master," a precybernetics science fiction tour de force; "The Death of Halpin Frayser," which is a fascinating treatment of the Oedipus complex; and "Moonlit Road," an experimental story told from three distinct points of view, one of them the thoughts of a dead man spoken through a medium.

It was Bierce's uncompromising honesty in portraying the world as he saw it that puts him above most other writers. His tragic and unflattering view of human existence is, if nothing else, his own unique vision. That he refused to accept the blind optimism of the day was to his everlasting credit. There were no rose-colored glasses, no uplifting "positive" thoughts on the nature of mankind— Bierce had been brave enough to say what he thought about the human condition in his newspaper work, and he felt he owed the same courtesy to the readers of his fiction. The convincingly terrifying visions put before us in *Can Such Things Be?* are all the more remarkable when you consider their lack of conventional character development, sparse descriptions and economy of line. He creates his own isolated vacuum of fear and terror, and the reader is dropped into it and left to fend for himself.

Bierce's attitude concerning the relative lack of critical praise for his second volume of stories is, as usual, best summed up in his own words:

> My how my fame rings out in every zone
> A thousand critics shouting, 'He's Unknown!'

6
DOMINION OVER
THE
ABSTEMIOUS

AROUND 1895 BIERCE DECIDED
to put some distance between himself and the bad memories in Saint
Helena and moved south to the tranquil hills overlooking Los Gatos.
Although his role of devil's advocate intimidated most people in the
town below he continued to receive a steady flow of San Francisco
disciples, who traveled to his mountain retreat to listen intently to
his literary theories and ask for his advice. One of the few locals who
found Bierce approachable and open was a widow in her thirties
named Una Hume. Charming and quickwitted, she became a good
friend of Bierce's, and he was often found at her magnificent ranch,
Glen Una, which served as one of the premier literary gathering
places in Northern California.

Once settled in Los Gatos the unpredictable Bierce switched
gears completely and, rather than basking in the limelight of his
latest book of short stories, channeled his considerable energies into
the "Prattle" column. After nearly ten years of writing the column
for the *Examiner,* Bierce, still recognizing Hearst's good newspaper
sense in picking talented men and staying clear of them, had nevertheless found much to detest in his politically opportunistic
employer. However, when the Congress debated a funding bill that
would cancel the Western railroads' indebtedness to the federal government for past land grants and loans, both Bierce and Hearst were

up in arms. Bierce's long-standing criticism of the Southern Pacific Railroad and its corrupt owners has already been mentioned, and Hearst was every bit as much in opposition to the Big Four. The difference between the two men was that Bierce's criticisms were based in ethical outrage whereas Hearst's opposition was politically motivated. In any case, the two agreed to join forces to wage an all-out war against their common enemy. The *Examiner* began its crusade against the so-called Funding Bill on the West Coast, and within a few months Hearst asked Bierce if he would take a special assignment in Washington, D.C., to lead the newspaper attack through the New York *Journal,* one of Hearst's latest newspaper acquisitions. In a classic case of two men working for the same cause with entirely different reasons, in January of 1896 Bierce packed his bags and left for Washington.

In Washington Bierce had at his disposal a crack staff of reporters, and he quickly worked out a plan of attack, which was based on a steady bombardment of dispatches and editorials printed in both the *Journal* and the *Examiner.* No doubt all of this turmoil was exceedingly embarrassing to publisher Hearst's father, Sen. George Hearst, whose close friend and political ally in Washington was Sen. Leland Stanford—Huntington's partner in the mismanagement of the Southern Pacific. Regardless, it was widely known that Collis P. Huntington was in Washington lobbying for the bill by buying votes in Congress. Opposed to outright repayment, the Big Four stood for gradual remission of the $75 million they owed the government by refunding with long-term, low interest bonds to mature in seventy-five years. People across the country let their feelings be heard; they were apprehensive of financial finagling as well as long-term bonds, and they voiced their fears that the devious Huntington was well on his way to yet another steal. It was Ambrose Bierce who stood up and spoke for the little man, and in the end it was a gross underestimation of Bierce's power as a journalist that led to Huntington's downfall. When Bierce wrote that "to hate rascality is my religion" the brain behind the railroad bloc didn't take him seriously. But after several months of amusingly critical columns and cynical outpourings concerning the Funding Bill, Huntington finally felt the Bierce sting. "Huntington Lying in his Last Ditch," read one of the his headlines, which proved to be considerably kinder than the opening sentence: "Mr. Huntington appeared before the committee and took his hands out of all pockets long enough to be sworn."

RAILROAD KING COLLIS P. HUNTINGTON AFTER THE 1896
DEFEAT OF HIS FUNDING BILL.

After six months of abuse Huntington simply broke under Bierce's methodical crusade in print and tried to pay off the annoying gadfly on the very steps of the nation's capitol.

"Name your price," Huntington said in a defeated tone. "Every man has his price."

"My price is $75 million," Bierce said loudly after a sizeable crowd had gathered, ". . . to be handed to the Treasurer of the United States."

That Bierce's greatest coup in journalism culminated in such a dramatic confrontation seemed too good to be true. He had single-handedly defeated the notorious Funding Bill and in doing so had

New York *Journal* political cartoonist James
Swinnerton showed both Bierce's intensity and
Collis P. Huntington's reaction to Bierce's
determination to kill the Funding Bill.

made a strong case for the public ownership of railroads. Although
this was a major journalistic victory and ultimately changed the
course of history, Bierce has gone virtually unrecognized for his contribution today. His rare gifts as an investigative reporter and incor-
ruptible columnist still stand as a model for modern journalists, but
his talents went further; Bierce also managed to transcend the limi-
tations of reporting by injecting his own keen wit and satirical
thrusts into his columns dealing with the railroad bloc. It was this le-
thal combination that ultimately defeated Huntington's Funding Bill.

After spending a year in Washington Bierce returned home to California something of a hero. Suffering from a complete physical breakdown brought about by stress, he spent several months at the old El Monte Hotel in Los Gatos trying to regain his health. He also found his spells of asthma increasingly difficult to cope with, and when they became especially severe he took the train to Wrights (a tiny settlement at the crest of the Santa Cruz Mountains), which

THE JEFFREYS HOTEL AT WRIGHTS IN THE SANTA CRUZ MOUNTAINS, TO WHICH BIERCE FREQUENTLY ESCAPED DURING THE 1890S TO FIND RELIEF FROM SEVERE ATTACKS OF ASTHMA.

afforded the warm, dry climate his condition required. It was during one of his periodic stays at the Jeffreys Hotel there that Bierce received the official word of Congress's order to the Southern Pacific Railroad to repay its government loan at six percent interest with twenty notes, one falling due each six months. The railrogues of the Southern Pacific would have to repay their debt in ten years instead of the eighty-three they had so carefully calculated.

AFTER THE DEFEAT

of the Funding Bill, Bierce was at the height of his reputation. As a crusading muckraker and an innovative literary genius his reputation soared to near-mythical proportions. During this period he con-

THE CYNIC IN HIS MID-FIFTIES WITH A COPY OF THE SAN
FRANCISCO *EXAMINER* ROLLED UP AND READY TO STRIKE.

tinued writing his "Prattle" column for Hearst while managing his
vast manuscript-reading service for his ever-growing circle of followers. However, there were disturbing signs of some of his loyal
disciples falling away—most notably Edwin Markham, who managed to get his poem "The Man with the Hoe" published in the
Examiner without Bierce's sponsorship. Having long encouraged
Markham, Bierce felt he held claim to his "discovery," so when Bailey
Millard, the literary editor of the Sunday *Examiner*, introduced
Markham's poem, Bierce was outraged. That one of his protégés

was brought to national attention by a fellow staff member was an unforgivable insult, and Bierce attacked the poet as a radical socialist and his poem as "seepage from the barnyard."

"The Man with the Hoe" was inspired by Millet's painting of the same title and is an honest and forthright tribute to the man who works with his hands. However, Bierce viewed it as an artful prolabor soapbox speech and felt his view was more than justified when the liberal Hearst seemed pleased at the nationwide acceptance of the poem. Bierce was extremely irritated; not only was his pupil brought before the public by someone else, but the antitrust sentiments of his employer were getting national attention, thereby encouraging Hearst to see himself as a viable presidential candidate. The Spanish-American War, often thought of as a Hearst-inspired conflict (fired by six-inch patriotic headlines complete with tricolored American flags waving on the front page) reinforced Bierce's opinion that his employer was a dangerous man politically. Bierce's own conception of American troops bullying this minor power in the interest of empire-building was unpopular with the *Examiner* readership, but he nevertheless stood up and voiced his misgivings in one of his columns during this period, and three-quarters of a century later the words seem to speak to us louder than ever:

We can conquer these people without half trying, for we belong to a race of gluttons and drunkards to whom dominion is given over the abstemious. We can thrash them consummately and every day of the week, but we cannot understand them; and is it not a great golden truth, shining like a star, that one does not understand {what} one knows to be bad?

While Bierce's reclusive nature made him a somewhat difficult man to track down, those fortunate enough to confront him at home, at his cabin in the Los Gatos hills, were usually surprised by his earthiness and love of wild animals. More often than not his guests would find themselves traipsing through the redwood forests to keep up with the hearty author. Yet even in the serenity of his mountain hideaway Bierce was plagued by problems with the *Examiner.* Whereas his agreement with Hearst was that there was to be no major tampering with his columns, he discovered that editors of other Hearst-owned papers across the country were picking up his "Prattle" columns as fillers for their editorial pages and indiscriminately cutting his copy to fit their needs. This highly unethical practice, coupled with Bierce's disdain of Hearst's increasingly liberal

bias in reporting, caused yet another of his growing number of resig-
nations on the premise that he could no longer permit himself to be
the pawn of "fools, fakers, and freaks." He was soon voicing his
opinion that Hearst had done more in the yellowing of journalism
than anyone else in the business and, as a result, newspapers were
becoming "indistinguishable from circus posters."

AMBROSE BIERCE ON A TREK THROUGH THE SOLITUDE OF
HIS BELOVED SANTA CRUZ MOUNTAINS.

As usual Bierce's resignation was rescinded within a few
weeks, after Hearst himself promised to clamp down on his editors'
tendency to condense the column. Satisfied for the moment, Bierce

agreed to continue his column, and shortly thereafter he took another bow, with the publication of a collection of his stories entit-led *Fantastic Fables*. Published by Putnam's in 1899, the book was actually a collection of 245 tales based on the Aesop method of story-telling with significant satirical twists, which had originally appeared in the London *Fun* magazine during Bierce's years of self-imposed exile in England. Typically they work on several levels:

THE OPOSSUM OF THE FUTURE

One day an Opossum who had gone to sleep hanging from the highest branch of a tree by the tail, awoke and saw a large snake wound about the limb, between him and the trunk of the tree.

"If I hold on," he said to himself, "I shall be swallowed; if I let go I shall break my neck."

But suddenly he bethought himself to dissemble.

"My perfected friend," he said, "my parental instinct recognises in you a noble evidence and illustration of the theory of development. You are the Opossum of the Future, the ultimate Fittest Survivor of our species, the ripe result of progressive prehensility – all tail!"

But the Snake, proud of his ancient eminence in Scriptural history, was strictly orthodox, and did not accept the scientific view.

It was also during this period that Bierce's friendship with Una Hume blossomed into a romance of sorts and he became a regular vis-itor at Glen Una, greeting and entertaining the salon of distin-guished literary guests who frequented the magnificent ranch. Sporting a huge swimming pool and beautiful stained glass windows throughout, this was a virtual shrine in the redwoods, and, here, many of the guests were surprised to find Bierce soft-spoken and gentle rather than the fuming bitter cynic one would expect to en-counter after reading his column. When fledgling authors whom he'd never met showed up with manuscripts to be evaluated, he treated all of them with impeccable manners regardless of the quality of their work.

Of course, it's also known that Bierce was far from a saint. Whether he held court at Glen Una or in his mountain cabin in Los Gatos, the generosity of the guidance he gave aspiring writers who sought him out for constructive criticism is qualified by the fact that he expected many of his female protégés to go to bed with him simply because he spent an hour correcting their misspellings or tidy-ing up their grammar. His decidedly warped view of women at the level of chattels had not changed over the years. Women as individuals, as people, he never attempted to understand. Bierce's attitudes followed the creed of his day, cautiously guarding the reputation of young girls of good social standing and viciously condemning the free-spirited emancipated woman. He respected the "good" woman but, in the finest of double-standard traditions, he gravitated toward the free-spirited souls, once writing "I have never been hard on women whose hearts go with their admiration, and whose bodies follow their hearts."

Around this time

one of George Sterlings's friends, a young student of architecture and aspiring poet named Herman Scheffauer, became one of Bierce's most prized students. After Bierce used some of Scheffauer's verse in his column the two men conspired to create a playful literary hoax, based on the stylistic resemblance of one of "Scheff's" unpublished

THE PRATTLER WITH PROTEGE HERMAN SCHEFFAUER
AND JULIE MILES IN LOS GATOS AROUND 1899.

poems, entitled "The Sea of Serenity," to some of Edgar Allen Poe's work. They managed to get the poem published in the *Examiner* in March of 1899 by claiming it was a lost Poe poem and therefore an important literary discovery, but Hearst's dramatic Spanish-American War headlines still dominated the public interest, and the literary deception fizzled miserably. Regardless, they soon became good friends on a student-teacher level, Scheff addressing him as "Thor" and Bierce loving every minute of it.

Scheffauer's poems, collected in *Of Both Worlds* and *Looms of Life,* failed to cause much of a stir in the literary community, yet he never compromised his sense of true art by turning to commercialism in recompense. He threw himself into writing several Grove Plays for the Bohemian Club's summer entertainments with the same abandon most thought he reserved for his serious poetry. In truth Scheffauer was the archetypical mad poet—sensitive, argumentative and free enough in spirit to seek out both extreme pleasure and intense pain for the sake of his work. Unfortunately he was not blessed with the talent to match his soaring poetic heart, and he ended his own life some years later in a state of depression over the cold reception of his poetry and Germany's defeat in World War I.

While still mentor to Scheffauer in 1899 Bierce, content to send his columns off to Hearst from his cabin, also continued his duties as critic and mentor to an ever-changing cast of female players. There was Lella Cotton, a shy poetess whom he literally ran into on his bicycle; young pupils with rosy cheeks, such as Eva Crawford and Mabel Wood; and the worldly sisters Kitty and Julie Miles. The master's jaunts into the Santa Cruz mountains usually included one or more of his starry-eyed disciples, a generous supply of his favorite brandy and white wine, books of poetry for instruction and a blanket to throw over the pine needles. Nearing sixty years of age, Bierce still had women throwing themselves at his feet, and at this point he didn't really care if it was his past journalistic outpourings, his fiction or his ruddy good looks that attracted them. One of the unprinted and presumably censored definitions in his "Devil's Dictionary" is supposed to have defined heaven as "copulation without culmination."

Late in 1899 Bierce made the mistake of objecting to some of Una Hume's society friends who frequented the ranch. The almost imperceptible shift in Hume's admiration away from Bierce and toward other, more contemporary literary luminaries who visited

---

her ranch told him that he was no longer in the center of her charmed circle. Rather than play second fiddle to anyone, he decided to make a characteristically flamboyant break from the salon. When Mrs. Hume stood her ground at Bierce's objections, he declared that Glen Una was a paradise "only during the closed season for snakes." And having smashed that friendship he proceeded to destroy yet another, picking a fight with Lella Cotton over some imagined slight. As in the past, Bierce's unstable nature and paranoid delusions contributed to a significant change in his life, which would shortly take place with seeming suddeness.

In October a huge forest fire burned everything on "Monte Paraiso"—the ranch owned by Bierce's good friend Josephine McCrakin. Suddenly he felt old and out of place. His habit of hoarding up insults, real and imaginary, took vent in an outbreak of arguments, disintroductions and angry letters sent to his old friends and new admirers alike. His impulse to wound those he once held close greatly reveals his vulnerable pride, yet it also shows him capable of coldly discarding like crumpled bits of waste paper friends who showed too much individuality or disagreed with his philosophy.

Bierce's monumental ego could not accept that his hold on the title of dean of West Coast literature was slipping. Having been urged for some time to join the staff of the New York *Journal*, he abruptly accepted the offer, on the condition that he live in Washington and be allowed to continue his "Prattle" column. He felt he had burned his bridges behind him in California and was more than ready for a change of scenery. By mid-December he was on a train heading east.

7
RETURN TO
THE ASHES

AMBROSE BIERCE ARRIVED

in Washington in January of 1900, and, much to his own surprise as well as that of those who knew him, he lived and worked in the nation's capital for the next ten years. While the first decade of the new century saw the miracle of flight at Kitty Hawk, Peary's conquest of the North Pole, the overnight acceptance of automobiles racing down the streets and the introduction of motion pictures, it also witnessed the downfall of Bierce as a man and a writer of fiction. Though still employed by Hearst and writing for the *Journal* as well as the *Examiner*, he realized that he had passed the peak of his creative career. At fifty-eight years old he decided to give up literature for journalism, and he spent his time in Washington as an unsympathetic watchdog of Congress and astute political reporter.

Then the roof fell in. In 1901 Bierce's talented second son, Leigh, seemingly lost touch with reality between his obsessions with drink and with women of questionable character. Formerly a respected journalist with a good deal of experience on the Los Angeles *Record*, Leigh had become a valued reporter on the New York *Telegraph* when he came down with pneumonia after a truly monumental spree during the holiday season. It seems that he became involved in delivering provisions to the needy in the spirit of Christmas and managed to become so potted en route that he gave away most of the donations before they reached their destination.

Tragically, Leigh's drunken episode also led to severe exposure, and the resulting pneumonia caused his death. Then some four years later, in 1905, Bierce's estranged wife Mollie died of heart failure in Los Angeles, where she had been living in seclusion with her aging mother for several years. Ironically, she had filed suit for divorce just a few months before her death because she was under the false impression that Ambrose wanted his legal freedom from her to remarry. Spiritually broken over the deaths of Mollie and Leigh, his existential belief that "nothing matters" again came crashing down on him.

Around this time his relations with Hearst were growing more strained than ever, and finally Bierce resigned from all newspaper work to devote his time to writing a column called "The Passing Show" for *Cosmopolitan*, a Hearst-owned magazine. Bierce's growing dislike of his employer during these years stemmed from Hearst's continued reliance on yellow journalism. Bierce's ambition in life, he half-joked, was to outlive the publisher for the supreme pleasure of howling over his grave. "If ever two men were born to be enemies he and I are they," he would later write. "Each stands for everything that is most disagreeble to the other, yet we never clashed . . . . Either congenitally or by induced perversity, he is inaccessible to the conception of an unselfish attachment or a disinterested motive . . . . nobody but God loves him and he knows it."

In 1908 publisher Walter Neale offered to bring out a twelve-volume set of Bierce's *Collected Works* that Bierce himself would edit, and the prospect of leaving a permanent monument to his journalistic and literary work thrilled the aging cynic. The following year, at the age of sixty-seven, Bierce realized that preparing his *Collected Works* was a truly herculean undertaking. Burdened with the exacting task of selecting and shaping the contents, he was finally forced to break all relations with Hearst in order to stay on schedule, devoting all his time to the job at hand. With the added pressure, however, Bierce became increasingly antisocial and suspicious. While he still liked his liquor and his ladies, it sometimes seemed the fun had gone out of both. His lifelong hobbies of bicycling, canoeing and hiking gave him more pleasure than socializing. In fact, his only real circle of friends was a group of old cronies at the Army and Navy Club in Washington. He all but turned his back on the literati in the East, and seemed content to shoot billiards and relive the

Civil War with high-ranking officers who addressed him as Major Bierce.

THIS PORTRAIT WAS BIERCE'S FAVORITE. IT WAS USED AS
THE FRONTISPIECE TO THE FIRST VOLUME OF
THE COLLECTED WORKS.

Early in 1910 Bierce was tiring of Washington and, now out from under the heavy Hearst thumb, began thinking about returning to California. Reminiscing about his worshipful pupils in the West, he thought particularly how he would enjoy visiting Sterling, Scheffauer and Carrington. Finally the plodding drudgery of pasting up copy for his *Collected Works* convinced him that he needed a change of scenery. Never a materialist, he sold his canoe and a few pieces of furniture in March and abruptly set out on the first leg of his journey, to New York. There he paused for a few weeks and attended several all-night farewell parties with publisher Walter Neale, later writing that the Big Apple was far too exhausting and cryptically adding that the city was nothing but "cocaine, opium and hashish." When sufficiently recovered from the festivities he finally set out again, interrupting the leisurely voyage with a three-day stopover in Panama, where he was entranced by the digging of the canal, and eventually reaching California.

UPON HIS ARRIVAL

in San Francisco on May 19, 1910, Bierce saw just enough of the scars made on his beloved city by the great earthquake and fire of 1906 to impulsively flee north to his brother Albert's cabin "Upshack," which overlooked the beautiful Russian River near Guerneville. At seventy years old, Albert, affectionately known as "Grizzly," had retired from his government position at the Mint in San Francisco and was enjoying the good life in Sonoma County. Settling in at the cabin with his brother, Bierce wrote to Neale in Washington:

It is paradise. Right above a beautiful river (we have a canoe) with a half-dozen pretty villages in sight below, and the woods already filled with their summer population from the city. One meets groups of pretty girls in camping attire everywhere – some of whom say that I held them on my knee when they were little (I mean to again), although I fancy it may have been their grandmothers.

Later in the spring Bierce made a nostalgic trip back to San Francisco. Greeted like a prodigal son, he was kept busy making the rounds at various dinners in his honor, but while the homecoming was enjoyable it was also vaguely depressing. It was impossible to resume old friendships after a decade in Washington because many of his old friends had either gone their own ways or died. Indeed, less than a month after his arrival in San Francisco Mark Twain died, and, as they had been contemporaries, the event weighed heavy on Bierce's mind. But more than this, he was forced to see and accept the truth that his long-held authority in the West had disappeared. He had become a curious literary fossil.

Just when Bierce felt he had lost touch with most of the California writers he was visited by his most famous pupil, George Sterling. It was an emotional reunion, and the two men spent several days visiting with the new crop of Bohemians around the San Francisco Bay. Sterling spared nothing to give his old master the grand tour, and rightly so, for it was Bierce who, in Washington in 1904, had received his pupil's two-hundred-line poem "A Wine of Wizardry" and had for the next several years waged a campaign to have it published. Meeting with rejections from all of the established magazines, a frustrated Bierce had finally managed to have the poem published in Hearst's *Cosmopolitan*, in 1907. Although the poem received national recognition and made other critics accept Sterling as a serious poet, "A Wine of Wizardry" was far from the masterpiece Bierce had labeled it, and his lofty praise whipped up a storm of controversy among critics who felt his judgment was a result of inability to separate the poet from the man. Regardless, Bierce remained a staunch supporter of Sterling's talent during his Washington years, and the poet was forever grateful.

Having established the famed writers' and artists' colony at Carmel in 1905, Sterling insisted that Bierce visit him there and meet some of the new literary flames now living and working in the beautiful central-coast hamlet. And when the master visited his former protégé, late that spring, a little old-fashioned Bierceian thunder lit up the shoreline community. To his way of thinking the "colony" was little more than "a nest of anarchists" posing as writers and artists. After lounging under the pines and eating abalone on the beach with the likes of novelist Mary Austin, writer-editor Harry Lafler, artist Xavier Martinez and short-story writer Jimmy Hopper, Bierce was convinced that it was a hotbed of socialism. When he later learned that writers Jack London and Upton Sinclair, whose literature often dealt with politics and economics, were also frequent visitors to the colony, Bierce dubbed Carmel the "home of cranks and curios." Since cottages in the colony rented for about ten dollars a month and good red wine could be bought for fifty cents a gallon, struggling artists and writers found Carmel a most hospitable place. The scenery was majestic and inspiring, the town was quiet, and there was intellectual stimulation available at the end of the day. However, Bierce soon concluded that drunken beach parties and prolonged hunting expeditions for young nymphs in the dreamy, fog-draped pine groves had become more important to Sterling than his work. Actually, Bierce was probably more upset with the free-love philosophy practiced in early Carmel than he was with Sterling's womanizing. Bierce was a staunch advocate of the art of male seduction, and he looked down upon the assertiveness and often blatant sexual advances initiated by some of the women in the art colony.

THE MAIN STREET IN CARMEL AROUND THE TIME OF BIERCE'S INFAMOUS VISIT TO THE ARTISTS' AND WRITERS' COLONY IN 1910.

While Bierce's objection to the Bohemian life-style, liberal politics and sometimes artificial artiness of the Carmel colony was made known in no uncertain terms, there were those in the group that were every bit as suspicious of his talent, and his conservative politics. Most felt they owed Bierce no allegiance. Many years later Mary Austin, in an article entitled "George Sterling at Carmel," wrote of Bierce:

I judged him to be a man secretly embittered by failure to achieve direct creation, to which he never confessed; a man of immense provocative power, always secretly—perhaps even to himself—seeking to make good in some other's gift what he had missed, always able to forgive any short-coming in his protégés more easily than a failure to turn out according to his prescription. I thought him something of a posturer, tending to over-weigh a slender inspiration with apocalyptic gestures.

SHORTLY AFTER HIS

irritating visit at the Carmel artists' colony Bierce escaped to the only unchanging refuge he knew he could count on—nature. With

Sterling, brother Albert and nephew Carleton he embarked on an extended camping trip to Yosemite and would later write that "as to the 'sights' to be seen, they are simply unspeakable. I haven't it in my heart to say a word about it." Sterling, however, had a little more to say about the trip, in his introduction to *The Letters of Ambrose Bierce* entitled "A Memoir of Ambrose Bierce":

I grew to know him better in those days, and he found us hospitable, in the main degree, to his view of things, socialism being the only issue on which we were not in accord. It led to many warm arguments, which, as usual, conduced nowhere but to the suspicion that truth in such matters was mainly a question of\taste.

ALTHOUGH THE DATE AND LOCATION OF THIS PHOTO ARE UNKNOWN, IT, NEVERTHELESS, PROVIDES A RARE GLIMPSE AT THE GENTLE SIDE OF THE GREAT CURMUDGEON.

Upon their return to the Bay Area Sterling, by now a central figure in San Francisco's Bohemian Club, invited fellow member Bierce to attend the Midsummer Bohemian High Jinks, just across the river and a couple of miles from Upshack. Since the early 1870s the Bohemian Club had served as a common meeting place for male writers, artists, actors and musicians in the city, and Bierce had been one of its earliest members. Shortly after the period of his active participation in the club it had acquired a picturesque grove of red-woods in Guerneville along the Russian River, some sixty miles to the north; it used this land for an annual two-week summer en-campment under the gigantic redwoods. Traditionally, the high point of the Jinks was the production of the annual Grove Play (always written, scored, designed and acted by members); however this particular midsummer celebration was overshadowed by the potentially awkward meeting of Bitter Bierce and Jack London – a match orchestrated by George Sterling.

IN THE SPRING OF 1901,

little more than a year after Bierce left for his decade-long residence in Washington, Sterling had first met London, the oyster pirate, sea rover and Klondike roustabout who had suddenly burst upon the literary scene as a gifted writer as well as an avid socialist. Before long Sterling's insecure need for an object of hero worship was trans-ferred to London, whose two novels, *The Call of the Wild* and *The Sea-Wolf* catapulted him to national fame. Joining a group of intellec-tual and gourmand Bohemians called the Crowd around the turn of the century in Piedmont, Sterling was soon introducing London to the pleasures of fine cooking, and London returned the favor by guiding the poet through the exotic world of Chinese brothels on the Barbary Coast.

When Sterling later deserted the Crowd in Piedmont to start the artists' and writers' colony in Carmel, London (after a few visits to the colony with his fiancée, Charmian Kittredge) opted for the life of a country gentlemen in the hills of Sonoma County at Glen Ellen. In 1905 the pressure exerted by the budding colony in Carmel to join its ranks weighed heavy on London, but in the end he felt that joining the seaside retreat would be a replay of his Bohemian days in Piedmont. Moreover, the overwhelming and cruel rejection of Charmian as a true member of the colony convinced him that he no longer felt the need to be one of the boys. He married Charmian in November, and the newlyweds later escaped to the seclusion of tiny Glen Ellen.

GEORGE STERLING, AT LEFT, AND JACK LONDON, AT
RIGHT, AROUND THE TIME OF THEIR EPIC DRINKING BOUT
WITH BIERCE AT THE BOHEMIAN GROVE IN 1910.

 Sterling's achieving unchallenged acceptance as the leader of
the Carmel colony in 1905 proved to be the only truly independent
action of his entire literary career. His slavish domination under
Bierce and, soon after, London, had by then fallen by the wayside.
However, some five years later he seized upon the opportunity of
arranging a meeting between the two titans by personally inviting
London (a member of the club since 1904) to attend the August, 1910,
High Jinks at the Bohemian Grove, which he knew Bierce would be
attending.

 Clearly Sterling was a great admirer of both men. But his motive for putting together the two writers, one of whom was known
to be an ardent socialist and the other known contentiously to label
anyone veering from the accepted political norm as an anarchist, is
still a matter of conjecture. Some biographers suggest that Sterling
set up the meeting to establish once and for all which man would be
his guru. Others think it was simply a mischievous prank. Regard-

less of his motive, in the summer of 1910 the chief players in this little drama were approaching the event quite differently.

While Bierce had spent most of the early summer leisurely canoeing on the Russian River and hiking in the woods around Guerneville, London had become despondent over the results of the July Fourth heavyweight boxing match held in Reno between the great white hope, Jim Jeffries, and the reigning title holder and first black heavyweight champion, Jack Johnson. A white supremacist, London covered the fight for the San Francisco *Chronicle*, and after Johnson knocked out Jeffries in the fifteenth round the paper's head-line read "Jack London Sees Tragedy in the Defeat of White Cham-pion." Moreover, London had lost a considerable amount of money by betting on Jeffries, and he was in a such a terrible mood over it that he was ready for a fight himself, writing to Charmian in late July about his impending meeting with Bierce: "Damn Ambrose Bierce. I won't look for trouble, but if he jumps me, I'll go him a few at his own game. I can play act and abuse just for the pure fun of it. If we meet, and he's introduced, I shall wait and watch for his hand to go out first. If it doesn't, hostilities begin right there."

WHEN THE TWO MEN

finally converged under the same roof at the Bohemian Club in August a nervous George Sterling thought better of the match up. "You mustn't meet him," the poet pleaded with Bierce, according to his own account of the tension-filled encounter. "You'd be at each other's throats in five minutes."

"Nonsense," said Bierce, already tipsy and leaning on the rustic redwood bar at the club, "bring him on. I'll treat him like a Dutch uncle."

As it turned out Bierce kept his word, for when a huge crowd of club members gathered around the bar to witness what they thought would be the English-language culmination of two cele-brated and opposing points of view, all they saw was a tentative introduction by Sterling, an outstreched hand offered by Bierce and London's acceptance of his open gesture of friendship. While the threat of actual physical combat was lessened by Bierce's uncharac-teristically warm greeting, most observers still stood at a safe dis-tance. There was no need to be leery. Bierce had somehow learned that Jack and Charmian's first child had died only a few days after birth several months earlier and had therefore decided in advance that things would be kept light. Having lost two grown children of his own, Bierce was sensitive to London's loss, although the subject was never brought up. Instead the two men matched each other drink for drink and gradually found they had more in common than they thought. Bierce had worked for William Randolph Hearst when the man had first broken into newspaper publishing after acquiring the *Examiner*, and London had done some brilliant reporting for the same newspaper while covering the Russo-Japanese War in 1904. Furthermore, their mutual damnation and total rejection of the artists' colony at Carmel created an odd intellectual bond. Bierce's comment that he would never want to be identified with Carmel because he was "warned by Hawthorne and Brook Farm" (a reference to Nathaniel Hawthorne's brief but disappointing association with an experimental art colony in West Roxbury, Massachusetts, in 1841) reflected exactly what London felt, and in fact one of London's novels published three years later, *The Valley of the Moon,* was his vindication of the choice to marry Charmian and live in isolated Glen Ellen.

While in the past Bierce had criticized Bohemians for their studied nonconformity and rejected the sentimental socialism of Jack London, he had been on record since the 1890s as favoring government ownership of railroads, prohibition of the importation of cheap labor, and some form of inheritance and progressive income taxes. His own definition of "radicalism" in *The Devil's Dictionary* as "the conservatism of tomorrow injected into the the affairs of today" explains London's later comment that if the cynic had been born a generation later he would have been a revolutionary socialist. Politics aside, the two writers proceeded to get so blitzed that Sterling and Arnold Genthe (the famed society photographer who also managed to capture the early Carmel years, as well as everyday scenes of the pre-1906 Chinatown in San Francisco) were forced to come to their aid. According to Genthe's autobiography, *As I Remember,* he and Sterling were forced to remove the two men to a nearby campsite, where the four of them sat around a roaring fire drinking and philosophizing until "none of us quite knew what we were talking about."

After several more hours of serious drinking the quartet demonstrated the degree of their inebriation by deciding to continue their alcoholic odyssey at Upshack, about two miles away. After crossing the dangerous Russian River in a rowboat the men stumbled along a set of railroad tracks that paralleled the river for a few hundred yards, then noticed Bierce had disappeared. Retracing their route while calling out his name, the three men finally spotted him at the bottom of a twenty-foot embankment. Evidently Bierce's derby hat had fallen off his head and rolled to the water's edge, and he had climbed down the steep slope to fetch it and decided to curl up in a soft fern bed for a short nap. When his companions woke him up he put on his derby, climbed back up the tracks and resumed the trek to his brother's cabin as if nothing had happened. Upon reaching Upshack Sterling promptly passed out, and Bierce and London continued to drink and talk the night away like long-lost buddies, each consuming a bottle of Three Star Martel in the process. The showdown everybody had hoped for had instead created an instant friendship between the two men, and the comic escapade is to this day considered one of the greatest drinking bouts in literary history.

8

THE ONLY
AVENUE
OF ESCAPE

DESPITE HIS SHENANIGANS

at the Bohemian Grove with London and Sterling, Ambrose Bierce felt oddly out of place in the California of 1910. Try as he would to recapture the spirit of the old days by attending dozens of literary luncheons and parties in San Francisco and Oakland, he was always faced with a grinding sense of anxiety. "San Francisco is not the same city that it was," he wrote Scheffauer:

Where are the courageous men of the Vigilante Committee of the old days? Where are those who broke the head of the mob with pick-handles in the time of Denis Kearney? I mean, where are those like them? It is clear that the business men and the professional men of today are no better than the labor unions and not half so brave.

Bierce's concern about San Francisco had as much to do with his own longevity as with any political or social climate. For him the Golden State he had once ruled over now seemed like an eerie gathering place for ghosts from his past. By October a vague restlessness grew out of his dissatisfaction, and he left California without a word of warning to his friends. After stopping over at the Grand Canyon for a few days of solitary hiking, he proceeded back to Washington, arriving on November fourth to discover that Walter Neale was extremely anxious for him to continue the editing of his

Collected Works. He subsequently suffered another serious attack of asthma, verbally abused some former friends for no discernable reason and invented a petty grievance to create a feud with the Army and Navy Club that resulted in his resignation. His extraordinary talent for attacking and cynically dissecting political injustice and social hypocrisy had finally degenerated into the non-productive bitterness of a crotchety old man.

Bierce's closest friends in Washington were two literary critics from Baltimore; the first was Percival Pollard, a critic for Colonel Mann's *Town Topics*. One of the first Eastern critics to praise Bierce's fiction, Pollard had always insisted that Bierce was the great neg-lected genius of American literature. The two men spent a good deal of time together in Washington as well as at Pollard's home in Baltimore and his summer place in Connecticut. And Pollard intro-duced Bierce to another of Mann's employees, the literary critic for *Smart Set,* the young H. L. Mencken. The resulting Bierce-Men-cken friendship was based on their mutual contempt for humanity and a shared delight in slashing apart novels they felt to be un-worthy of publication. Mencken's debt to Bierce was acknowledged in many of his writings, most of them making the point that Bierce was the only genuine wit produced in America. In later years he would write about Bierce's bleak view of humanity in *Prejudices: Sixth Series:*

So far in this life, indeed, I have encountered no more thorough-going cynic than Bierce was. His disbelief in man went even further than Mark Twain's: he was quite unable to imagine the heroic, in any ordinary sense. Nor, for that matter, the wise. Man, to him, was the most stupid and ignoble of animals. But at the same time the most amusing. Out of the spectacle of life about him he got an unflagging and Gargantuan joy. The obscene farce of politics delighted him. He was an almost amorous connoisseur of theology and theologians. He howled with mirth when-ever he thought of a professor, a doctor or a husband.

Mencken's personal view of the old cynic may have been slightly tainted by the unsettling experience of attending the funeral of Percival Pollard with Bierce in the winter of 1911. The elder critic had been forced to undergo brain surgery earlier in the year and had suffered a horrendous and agonizingly slow death. Deeply affected by Pollard's passing, Bierce's dual nature allowed him to give vent to his famed cynicism in front of a horrified Mencken as the two shared the same carriage following the cremation. According to Mencken's own account of the sad afternoon, he was shocked to the bone as he listened glassy eyed to Bierce's macabre suggestion that Pollard's ashes should be moulded into bullets and shot at publishers.

Having visited Bierce in the East at Sag Harbor the summer before Pollard's death, George Sterling somehow now convinced his old mentor to give California another chance. After sufficiently recovering from the loss of his friend and touring some old Civil War battlefields in Richmond, Virginia, Bierce arrived in California in June of 1912 for what proved to be his final visit. Settling in Oakland for a time, he again made the rounds within the Bay Area, and also stayed at Upshack with his brother Albert. Yet the fanfair of his 1910 visit was clearly missing, and the second pilgrimage quickly proved to be a disappointment. For four months he tried in vain to make a success out of his sentimental journey, but in the end he knew it had been a mistake. Nothing had changed – California was simply going to hell. With labor unions, woman's suffrage, socialism and the newest bit of "white magic" to hit the Golden State, Christian Science, he felt like he was in a foreign land. Feeling the assault of change, Bierce soon took the offensive and, after refusing an invitation to Carmel offered by Sterling, the old master went about picking apart his former pupil. Sterling's growing socialist leanings and his free-love philosophy, which ultimately caused his wife's suicide, finally became too much for Bierce. He ended their friendship by deliberately picking a fight with the poet, and his last letter of disintroduction addressed him as "Great Poet and Damned Scoundrel." Sterling was crushed by the letter and years later wrote that the tone of Bierce's tirade was that of "God talking to a gutter-snipe."

After a round of

final goodbyes in October of 1912 Bierce turned his back on California, never to return. The following year was spent in Washington, and most of his time was devoted to defending his twelve-volume *Collected Works*, which was not well received by the critics. While some of the volumes (especially those containing his fiction and better journalistic work) were applauded, the handsomely bound set as a whole failed miserably. Stubbornly shunning editorial assistance or even the advice of an impartial reader, Bierce's vain and overwhelming desire for literary eminence had resulted in an imbalanced hodgepodge of writings, including much that was of a temporary nature or simply too localized. The relative success of his short stories reprinted in the first few volumes, and even of volume seven, *The Devil's Dictionary*, was not enough to salvage the complete set. As had happened so many times in the past, the un-yielding nature of Bierce's personality had worked against him, for an editor with any degree of impartiality and emotional distance from the writings could have compiled a far more impressive collection in half as many volumes.

In 1913 Bierce's world slowly crumbled under him. At seventy-one years of age he was a physical wreck from the combined effects of asthma and alcohol, emotionally distraught by the poor sales of his *Collected Works* and feeling increasingly uncomfortable in the East. His life was in a tailspin, and it seemed regardless of where he was living he soon became anxious and yearned to be somewhere else. In February when one of the last members of the old guard, Joaquin Miller, died in Oakland, he felt all the more like a literary relic. Alone in the nation's capital he began wondering whether his favorite character, the grim reaper, had cruelly foresaken him.

After months of depression that culminated in a series of violent rages aimed at his few remaining friends, Bierce announced his bizarre decision to travel south—to observe the ongoing revo-lution in Mexico. According to Carey McWilliam's full-length 1929 study *Ambrose Bierce: A Biography,* the aged author visited his only surviving child, Helen, in Bloomington, Illinois, and left with her for safekeeping a large collection of his personal papers, after discussing the reasons for his perilous journey south:

Why should I remain in a country that is on the eve of woman's suffrage and prohibition? . . . In America you can't go east or west any more, or north, the only avenue of escape is south. I'm going back to Washington and make preparations to leave. I'll take some letters along with me and strike the border near El Paso. It will be easy enough to get along. I'm going to buy a donkey and hire a peon. I can see what's doing; perhaps write a few articles about the situation; and then pass on to the west coast of Mexico. From there I can go to South America, cross the Andes and ship to England. This fighting in Mexico interests me. I want to go down there and see if the Mexicans can shoot straight.

Upon his return to Washington Bierce put his affairs in order and wrote a handful of mysterious farewell letters, the most perplexing of which was sent to his brother Albert in Guerneville and was said to have been so brutally honest about Ambrose's impending doom that it kept Albert from sleeping and haunted his soul to the point where he lost his health, suffered a stroke of apoplexy and, within five months, himself died. The most ominous of these letters, however, was written to Bierce's nephew's wife, Lora, and read in part:

If you should hear of my being stood up against a Mexican stone wall and shot to rags please know that I think it is a pretty good way to depart this life. It beats old age, disease or falling down the cellar stairs. To be a Gringo in Mexico—ah, that is euthanasia!

Bierce finally left Washington early in October of 1913. Traveling by rail, he arrived in Chattanooga the following day and spent a week exploring the Civil War battlefields of his past—visiting Chickamauga, Shiloh, Nashville and Kenesaw Mountain. Moving on, before the end of the month he reached New Orleans, where he was caught in a storm and laid up for several days with asthma. While recuperating he granted interviews to some local reporters and

DRAPED IN THE AMERICAN FLAG, HERE THE SEVENTY-
ONE-YEAR-OLD AMBROSE BIERCE IS PICTURED DURING HIS
SENTIMENTAL 1913 TRIP THROUGH THE CIVIL WAR
BATTLEFIELDS OF HIS YOUTH.

Ambrose Bierce

openly discussed his retirement and his ultimate goal of reaching England via South America. When one of the reporters from the *States* asked him why a man of his years would risk taking such a dangerous journey into war-torn Mexico Bierce was as assertive as he'd been in his letters, this time saying "I like the game. I like the fighting. . . . I want to see it."

Pushing on into Texas Bierce reached San Antonio on the twenty-seventh, where he was received like a foreign ambassador by the cavalry officers at Fort Sam Houston and was entertained for another week. Finally, on November sixth, he reached the border at Laredo. His plan to cross the border into Mexico and join the forces of Pancho Villa and his rebellion against the newly established government of General Huerta was postponed when yet another attack of asthma halted his progress. When Bierce regained his strength he departed and, in a letter to Carrie Christiansen, mentioned leaving a trunk containing some books and a manuscript in the storage room of the Laredo hotel in which he was staying. According to Helen Bierce the manuscript was actually a recently completed exposé-type biography of none other than William Randolph Hearst. Although Bierce had secretly worked on the biography intermittently for several years he had no intention of seeking out a publisher until the death of his subject's mother, Phoebe Apperson Hearst, whom he had greatly admired for three decades. This book, which would have been an invaluable insider's look at the politically ambitious publishing magnate, never saw the light of day. The trunk mysteriously disappeared from the hotel in Laredo without a trace less than a year after Bierce's departure, and Phoebe Hearst didn't die until 1919, the year her famous son began construction on his dream castle overlooking the Pacific at San Simeon.

From letters now in the manuscript collection at the Huntington Library in San Marino, California (an institution that houses the finest collection of Bierceiana in the country and, ironically, was founded by the nephew of his most hated enemy—Collis P. Huntington), it is known that Bierce's next stop was El Paso. From there he crossed the border into Juarez in late November and somehow received credentials as an observer attached to Pancho Villa's revolutionary army. Then he traveled to Chihuahua on horseback, and wrote his last letter to his devoted secretary in Washington, Carrie Christiansen. Postmarked Chihuahua City and dated December 26,

1913, it read: "Trainload of troops leaving Chihuahua every day. Expect next day to go to Ojinaga, partly by rail."

These were the last words ever received from Ambrose Bierce. His brief message written the day after Christmas was destined to echo down the halls of literary history. In creating his own mysterious exit he swung the door open for theories both logical and

IN THE END, THE AGED MISANTHROPE WAS LEFT ON HIS OWN TO SEEK OUT HIS FATE IN REVOLUTIONARY MEXICO.

Ambrose Bierce

crackpot as to how, when and where he met his end. After years of Secret Service investigations, Pinkerton searches, official U.S. Army inquiries and even consultations with mediums who were thought to have had communications from the spirit realm, the unexplained disappearance of Ambrose Bierce came to be considered one of the great vanishments of the modern world. From the time of his presumed death people who had never read a word of Bierce's newspaper work or fiction were suddenly intrigued with his fate.

Writers, in particular, have now found fascination in the Bierce mystery for seventy years. Since his superb disappearance act a wide spectrum of theories have been put forward; from his death in the battle of Ojinaga to a natural death following complications brought on by one last bout with asthma; from his suicide by throwing himself into the Grand Canyon to his death at an advanced age in the insane asylum at Napa. Bierce's fate has become an odd literary parlor game, but the fact remains that everything beyond his last letter from Chihuahua is pure speculation. All theories fail for lack of evidence.

AFTERWORD

THE EXACT MANNER
and moment of Bierce's death is not important. That his eccentric life and mysterious death have sometimes overshadowed his work is a shame. Lionized in the West and generally neglected in the East during his lifetime, his reputation and accomplishments are now coming into sharper focus. Bierce was one of the greatest wits ever produced in America. His uncompromising satire was of a breed all its own, and greatly influenced a host of modern writers. For dec-ades the weelky journalistic thunderbolts of ridicule he issued from various mountain retreats found their mark and exposed fools, political crooks and hypocrisy in California. Bierce's all-but-forgotten contribution in singlehandedly defeating Huntington's unjust Funding Bill was probaby his greatest journalistic victory and remains an amazing testament to the power wielded by his pen. Grossly underestimated as a journalist, it took Bierce's home state of Ohio three-quarters of a century to pay tribute to his unique talent by inducting him into the School of Journalism's Hall of Fame at Ohio State University, in April of 1983. California, and in particular the city of San Francisco, has been even more negligent in formally acknowledging his tremendous contributions.

Bierce's hilariously grim and sardonic definitions in *The Devil's Dictionary*, addressed to "enlightened souls who prefer dry wines to sweet, sense to sentiment, wit to humor, and clean English to slang," are to this day used by people who have absolutely no idea of their source. In its own twisted way the book is a work of genius and the least dated of all his writings. One generation after another has turned to it as the ultimate reference book, to be read during particularly cynical hours as well as for sheer entertainment.

As for Ambrose Bierce's contribution to American literature, in recent years, it has been looked upon in a more favorable light than in Bierce's own era. Critics appraising his fictional output in the past often called attention to his inability to create believable characters and to his cold, unsympathetic tone. Today, however, Bierce is increasingly looked upon as a flawed genius whose faults ultimately set him apart from the mainstream of fiction writers. In his collection of Civil War stories, *Tales of Soldiers and Civilians,* now better known under its British title *In the Midst of Life,* he bravely denied the heroism of the war and forced the view that during this terrifying conflict life was cheap and death simply meaningless. While his contemporaries slanted their fiction toward an identified readership, Bret Harte painting picturesque Wild West scenes aimed at quenching the seemingly insatiable appetite for "authentic" western outlaw stories and Mark Twain relying on the tall-tale brand of humor, Bierce stubbonly refused to sell out during the Gilded Age, and faced the facts in his fiction. The Civil War and the lawlessness on the Western frontier – something he knew more about than both other writers combined – spelled murder, plain and simple.

Bierce's stories of horror and the supernatural, with their cruel and ironic twists, represent about one-half of his fictional output. The best of these brilliantly haunting tales stand up well even when compared to Poe, H. P. Lovecraft and today's masters of the genre. His deep inner torment and taste for the grotesque have placed him forever on the dark side of American literature, and today he is considered by many to be the true father of black humor. His love of the outré and the absurd have come full circle – the times have finally caught up with Bitter Bierce, and his stature in literature will grow in importance rather than diminish. While it is unlikely that he will ever achieve any degree of general popularity, due to the narrow appeal of the reality he portrayed (and even the old cynic himself would spout "Thank God" and "Amen" to this), in the future a genuine grass-roots Bierceian revival may well evolve. His fears and anxieties concerning the true nature of man are what many today feel but are afraid to face. As a sense of hopelessness centering on the threat of a nuclear holocaust or chemical annihilation becomes more real with each passing decade, the existential black humor and satirical epigrams of Ambrose Bierce will speak ever louder and more clearly.

SELECTED BIBLIOG-RAPHY

Atherton, Gertrude. *Adventures of a Novelist.* New York: Liveright, Inc., 1932.

Bierce, Helen. "Ambrose Bierce at Home." *The American Mercury,* no. 120 (December 1933), 453–58.

Castro, Adolphe de. *Portrait of Ambrose Bierce.* New York; The Century Co., 1920.

Fatout, Paul. *Ambrose Bierce, the Devil's Lexicographer.* Norman: University of Oklahoma Press, 1951.

Ferlinghetti, Lawrence and Nancy J. Peters. *Literary San Francisco.* San Francisco; City Lights Books, 1980.

Genthe, Arnold. *As I Remember.* New York: Reynal and Hitchcock, 1936.

Grattan, C. Hartley. *Bitter Bierce.* New York: Doubleday, Doran and Co., 1929.

Kingman, Russ. *A Pictorial Life of Jack London.* New York: Crown Publishers, Inc., 1979.

Lewis, Oscar. *Bay Window Bohemia.* New York: Doubleday and Co., 1956.

———. *The Big Four.* New York: Alfred A. Knopf, 1938.

McWilliams, Carey. *Ambrose Bierce: A Biography.* New York: A. C. Boni, 1929.

Mencken, H. L. *Prejudices: Sixth Series.* New York: Alfred A. Knopf, 1927.

Neale, Walter. *Life of Ambrose Bierce*. New York: Walter Neale, 1929.

Noel, Joseph. *Footloose in Arcadia*. New York: Carrick and Evans, 1940.

O'Connor, Richard. *Ambrose Bierce: A Biography*. Boston: Little, Brown and Co., 1967.

Older, Mrs. Fremont. *William Randolph Hearst, American*. New York: D. Appleton-Century Co., 1936.

Pollard, Percival. *Their Day in Court*. New York: Neale Publishing Co., 1909.

Sterling, George. "Introduction." *In the Midst of Life*. New York: Modern Library, 1927.

―――. "A Memoir of Ambrose Bierce," Introduction to *The Letters of Ambrose Bierce*. Edited by Bertha Clark Pope. San Francisco: The Book Club of California, 1922.

Swanberg, William A. *Citizen Hearst*. New York: Charles Scribner's Sons, 1961.

Walker, Franklin. *San Francisco's Literary Frontier*. New York: Alfred A. Knopf, 1939.

―――. *Ambrose Bierce, the Wickedest Man in San Francisco*. San Francisco: The Colt Press, 1941.

―――. *The Seacoast of Bohemia: An Account of Early Carmel*. San Francisco: The Book Club of California, 1966.

Wilson, Edmund. *Patriotic Gore*. New York: Oxford Press, 1962.

BOOKS BY AMBROSE BIERCE

Bierce, Ambrose. *Black Beetles in Amber*. San Francisco: Western Authors Publishing Co., 1892.

―――. *Can Such Things Be?* New York: Cassell Publishing Co., 1893.

―――. [Dod Grile, pseud.]. *Cobwebs from an Empty Skull*. London: Routledge and Sons, 1874.

―――. *The Collected Works*. 12 vols. New York and Washington: Neale Publishing Co., 1909–1912.

―――. *The Cynic's Word Book*. New York: Doubleday, Page and Co., 1906.

―――― [William Herman, pseud.]. *The Dance of Death*. San Francisco: Henry Keller and Co., 1877.

―――. *Fantastic Fables*. New York: G. P. Putnam's Sons, 1899.

―――. [Dod Grile, pseud.]. *The Fiend's Delight*. London: Hotten, 1872.

————. *The Monk and the Hangman's Daughter,* with C. A. Danziger. Chicago: F. J. Schulte, 1892.

———— [Dod Grile, pseud.]. *Nuggets and Dust.* London: Chatto and Windus, 1872.

————. *The Shadow on the Dial.* Edited by S. O. Howes. San Francisco: A. M. Robertson, 1909.

————. *Shapes of Clay.* San Francisco: W. E. Wood, 1903.

————. *Tales of Soldiers and Civilians.* San Francisco: E. L. G. Steele, 1891.

————. *Write It Right.* New York and Washington: Neale Publishing Co., 1909.

INDEX